# THE COPARENTING MANIFESTO

## PRACTICAL TOOLS TO LOWER STRESS AND IMPROVE COOPERATION

Jon C Peters, MSW

Copyright © 2012 Jon Peters

All rights reserved. Copyright under Berne Copyright Convention, Universal Copyright Convention, and Pan-American Copyright Convention. No part of this book may be reproduced, stored in a retrieval system, or transmitted in any form, or by any means, electronic, mechanical, photocopying, recording or otherwise, without prior permission of the author.

ISBN: 1479339032
ISBN-13: 978-1479339037

## DEDICATION

I am grateful to have had the opportunity to go to hell with hundreds of parents who struggle to co-parent their children through confusing and challenging life situations. Bless you for your courage and perseverance. And, I am deeply thankful for my former wife, Yara, and our beautiful, exuberant daughter, Ysabel, for teaching me the value of being the best father and co-parent I can be.

# CONTENTS

**1 THINKING ABOUT COPARENTING**     1
*Here's the Plan*     4
*The Ideal Co-parenting Relationship*     7

**2 THIS IS YOUR BRAIN ON DIVORCE**     10
*The Physical Stress Response*     10
*A Sense of Control*     11
*Know that you are stressed*     12
*Generally lower your stress level*     14
*The Negative Lens through Which You View the Other Parent*     16
*Losing Perspective*     16
*Be Conscious of the Green Slice to Keep Positivity In Play*     19
*Create the Green Slice*     20
*Fast and Slow Thinking*     27
*Know When the Building is on Fire, and When It Isn't*     27
*My Ex is Evil, Stupid, and Crazy!*     32
*Ghosts or Artifacts from the Past*     34
*Losing Sight of Innocent Bystanders*     36
*Question Reality*     37

**3 ANTIDOTES TO TROUBLED THINKING**     41
*Levels of Response*     42
*Get Good Sleep*     47
*Reduce Your Caffeine Intake*     50

**4 TOP 6 STRATEGIES**     51
*Top Strategy One: Clarification*     51
*Top Strategy Two: Time-out*     53

| | |
|---|---|
| Top Strategy Three: Thankfulness | 55 |
| Top Strategy Four: Empathy | 57 |
| Top Strategy Five: Focus on the Present, Not the Past | 60 |
| Top Strategy Six: Pay Attention to The BIG TRIGGER! | 65 |

## 5 HANDLING CHALLENGING EMOTIONS — 68

| | |
|---|---|
| Sadness | 69 |
| Guilt | 70 |
| Anger | 71 |
| Be Aware of Your Anger | 72 |
| Identify the Should | 75 |
| Avoid Sarcasm | 77 |
| The Other Parent's Emotions | 78 |
| Dealing with the Other Parent's Sadness | 79 |
| Don't Ignore the Other Parent's Anger | 80 |
| Ignore the Other Parent's Anger | 82 |
| Be Trustworthy | 84 |
| Don't Attack Your Child When Triggered by the Other Parent | 88 |
| Fan the Flames, and You Will Get Burned | 90 |

## 6 BETTER COMMUNICATION 101 — 94

| | |
|---|---|
| Dial up Structure: Use Live Communication Less | 94 |
| When Possible, Prepare Ahead of Time | 98 |
| Be Brief: Avoid Communication Bundles | 99 |
| Use Clean Language | 100 |
| Stop Complaining | 102 |
| Avoid Universals: Be Specific | 104 |
| Use "and" instead of "but" | 104 |
| Communicate about Things that Matter to the Other Parent | 105 |
| Don't Communicate Through Your Child | 106 |
| Talking to Your Child on the Phone | 108 |
| Have the Process Conversation | 110 |

## 7 DOING CONFLICT WELL — 114

| | |
|---|---|
| During Conflicts, Focus on the Goal AND the Future Relationship | 119 |
| Focus on the Issue, Not the Person | 122 |

## 8 DEALING WITH THE LEGAL SYSTEM — 124

| | |
|---|---|
| *How Did We Get into This Mess?* | *125* |
| *When Can Our Child Decide Custody?* | *127* |
| *Parental Alienation Syndrome* | *132* |
| *Father's Rights* | *133* |
| *So, Should We Get A Custody Evaluation?* | *134* |
| *Will Therapy Help Our Co-parenting Relationship?* | *138* |
| *What if Others Get Involved in Our Case?* | *140* |
| *Should We Use Mediation?* | *143* |
| *Another Way to Avoid the Adversarial Legal Process* | *144* |
| **9 STRESS MANAGEMENT TECHNIQUES** | **145** |
| *Dealing with General Stress* | *146* |
| *Dealing with Short-Term Spikes of Stress* | *147* |
| *Counting* | *149* |
| *Take a Deep Breath* | *150* |
| *Calming Words* | *151* |
| *Walking Meditation* | *152* |
| *Sitting Meditation* | *153* |
| *Gratitude* | *154* |
| **10 TYING IT ALL TOGETHER** | **155** |

# ACKNOWLEDGMENTS

Thanks to my friend, Nicole Johnson, for her *waiting for the bus* metaphor. Back cover photo: Yara Cluver.

# 1 THINKING ABOUT CO-PARENTING

Fifteen years ago I had the wonderful opportunity to work in a program which supported separated parents involvement in their children's lives and aimed to help them co-parent more effectively. This led me into a career focus that I had not previously considered. Over the years, I have continued to work with separated parents—and their children—as a divorce mediator, counselor, custody evaluator, parent coordinator, and psychotherapist. I have consulted to legal proceedings and have served as an expert witness in divorce and paternity hearings. I began this work fresh out of graduate school fueled by some compassion and much idealism. Luckily, my clients helped me wake up to reality and get on with developing some practical skills.

Unfortunately, many parents engage in seemingly endless conflict after separation. In fact, one-third of parents are still litigating their divorces five years post-separation. One-fourth are still litigating at six years. Regardless of the causes for such lengthy, costly, and damaging litigation, millions of parents are locked in unsatisfying conflict and their children are suffering. I have mostly worked with these high-conflict parents. Probably seventy percent of my clients have been involved with the courts in one way or another and many arrive at my office due to a court order to do so.

Many parents read books about divorce and understand what they *should* do. It isn't difficult to see how parental conflict is bad for children. But, they may feel like failures when attempting to steer toward a more positive co-parenting relationship. The existing resources are mostly preachy and idealistic without providing tools that address the complications of post-separation co-parenting. Court-mandated divorce education classes tend to merely skim the surface of a wide range of divorce issues and don't provide communication and conflict-resolution skills. It is understandable that these classes have limitations. Only so much material can be covered in four hours (I know as I have taught over two hundred such classes). But, however useful such material may be, parents must face the complications of their situation. And, many parents have complained that available divorce books fail to provide enough specific guidance to reduce post-separation conflicts.

I have enjoyed working with these parents. Over the years, I have developed strategies to help them craft a functional co-parenting relationship in which they rely on each other (not therapists, attorneys, or the courts) to accomplish shared parenting. It has been a joy for me to help parents deal with post-separation issues and keep their children out of the middle of their conflicts. Do they all achieve an ideal co-parenting relationship? No. Many of them are dealing with life situations that have complications that are durable and not easily solved. But, there is so much value in reducing a large part of the post-divorce stress and constructively communicating and cooperating.

This is not a book primarily focused on how to help your children cope with your separation. Some of this content does relate directly to how you effectively parent your children as separated parents. However, the primary focus is on how to craft the optimal co-parenting relationship. I believe that several good books have provided parents with insights and strategies to respond to children's needs after divorce. My favorite is *Mom's House Dad's House* by Isolina Ricci. And, state-required divorce education classes typically help parents be more aware of how to respond effectively to their children's needs through and after divorce. I believe there is a need to address the complexity of transitioning into workable co-parents.

This book distills fifteen years of experience working with separated parents. I offer practical advice about how to make the transition into being constructive, cooperative co-parents whether you are newly separated or have been struggling to improve your co-parenting for years. Because I have been in therapeutic and mediating roles with divorcing clients, I have had to respond to immediate, critical situations. Preaching ideals was of little value to parents who were soon headed to court or who were fighting to the point of having Child Protective Services threaten to remove their children. So many parents know what good co-parenting looks like, but are confused about how to achieve it. Fortunately, there are valuable strategies that make it more likely you will be able to steer yourself in that direction and reduce your, and your children's, stress.

I aim to be practical. I invite my clients to fire me as soon as possible. I prefer to work myself out of a case as soon as possible. This book is the culmination of that brief-therapy approach. I work this way with my clients because their lives take place outside, not in, my office and they are focused on important issues which need to be addressed sooner, not later. I believe you can benefit from these gems my clients have helped me gather.

This book addresses issues of perception that affect everyone and which are particularly unhelpful for separated parents. It covers issues of communication and conflict resolution. And, it will cover many typical issues that are pitfalls for separated parents. In a later section of the book, I offer a variety of stress-management techniques because, as I will explain in the opening chapters, high stress sabotages our brains and steers us into unnecessary conflict.

You may not be feeling highly hopeful right now. That's OK. Hope won't help you much if it's not based on actually doing things better. A much more valuable hope will form when your co-parenting relationship improves. Trust yourself and have courage to experiment with the challenges and complications of separated co-parenting. This book will help you see how to make those positive changes.

I don't want to be another professional making parents feel like failures by simply explaining that they are doing things wrong. So many divorce books and well-intentioned therapists give rich explanations of how post-separation conflict will harm children emotionally—as though parents weren't already motivated to protect their children! And, they preach ideals with little practical advice about what to do when you can't get along. I have found joy in celebrating the strengths of my clients, even when they are faced with frustrating complications. I am enlivened to offer practical strategies for dealing with the intricacies of interpersonal conflict. If your car were broken down on the side of the road, you'd be annoyed if someone slowed down enough just to preach that you should have bought a better car. You'd be happy if your mechanic friend stopped to actually help you fix it. The many parents I've worked with have helped me to become that mechanic.

*Here's the Plan*

Good intentions and wishful thinking are worth something. But, so often, they fall short of solving complications. As I explained earlier, it is easy to imagine vague ideals related to co-parenting. And, yet, those ideals seem to go out the window in moments of conflict and confusion, especially when you are stressed and emotionally triggered. Things get derailed. When this happens repeatedly, you may lose hope that it can ever improve or worry that it won't improve quickly enough for you and your children.

My own good intentions didn't seem to be worth much, either, when clients were in my office angry, confused, and wanting something to help them steer out of unsatisfying conflict. A more helpful approach would be to transform ineffective arguing into constructive interactions. You have chosen to devote some time to read this book. So, I will reward you with some practical strategies for navigating those moments of conflict. I trust that you already have ideas about what a better co-parenting relationship will look like. And, you are more expert on your children and your particular situation than I could ever be. So, let me offer a map for some of the territory that tends to be most confusing: the part about reducing unhelpful conflict and increasing cooperation. I trust you'll figure out the rest.

The first part of my plan is to educate you on how stress shifts perceptions. It is no news to you that divorce is stressful. There is no magic wand to wave to get rid of that stress. Sorry. However, the good news is that understanding the ways that stress effects your perceptions and reactions can be of great benefit. This is because these effects are predictable. Our brains are wired to have some specific stress reactions. If we know what those stress-related shifts are, we can correct for them. You will learn to recognize the shifts that happen during post-separation conflict and how to manage them so that they have much less effect on your interactions with your other parent and your children. If you dial this stress out of the equation, the helpful capacities of your brain can stay online and help you steer toward a more ideal co-parenting relationship.

Another aspect of high stress is challenging emotions. You are dealing with your personal grief as well as having strong empathy for your children's stress and grief. You are also experiencing the emotions of past, unresolved conflicts. And, you are having current, ongoing interactions with the other parent many of which result in challenging emotions. You may be looking for the "off" button about now! Unfortunately, there is no such button and I caution you from trying to push it (say, through drinking or drugging because of the risks and costs of those strategies). But, I do have some ideas about what you can do about those strong emotions and how to keep them from derailing your better intentions.

I will offer advice around making the transition to being co-parents. There are some predictable pitfalls that parents face and knowing about them and correcting for them will set you up for success. Failing to be successful marriage partners doesn't mean you are doomed to fail as co-parents. And, the artifacts of past failures and hurts don't need to prevent you from forming a workable co-parenting relationship. I will explain how. I will also explain what to do when you screw up—it will happen!

Because good communication matters, I will offer some ideas about how to communicate in a clear, civil manner that serves your co-parenting relationship. Again, you may not feel very hopeful about this if you have a history of all, or most, communications with your ex resulting in unsatisfying conflict. However, this can change. And, it can change even if it seems that your ex is not on board with the plan. In addition to communication skills, I will help you understand conflict resolution skills—how the process is as important as the content of your conflicts.

Because many parents focus on litigation as a means of resolving conflict, I will offer my perspective on the difference between legal and non-legal issues and why you should avoid going to court when other means of conflict resolution could be more helpful. I will also explain why children should be kept out of the court process and address issues that sometimes result in children being put in the middle of legal matters. I will also explain how to consider mediation as a means for avoiding costly and damaging litigation.

Lastly, I will offer some stress management techniques. Lowering your stress is very important. First, you need to feel less stressed as soon as possible. It will be good for you and for your relationship with your children. And, you need to lower the effect that stress is having on your co-parenting relationship. This will be explained in the next few chapters. But, I think this is the biggest reason for such lasting post-separation hostility. Stress remains high which triggers more dysfunctional reactions and those hostile interactions provide plenty of stress to keep the cycle going. Understanding how that happens and doing proactive strategies to dial that stress out of the equation is one of the most helpful things you can do for yourself and your co-parenting relationship.

*The Co-Parenting Manifesto* is about process—*how* you perceive and react—rather than *content*, or substance, in your situation. It is about achieving a state of body and mind conducive to functional co-parenting. You need to lower stress in your body and clear your mind of some predictable and unhelpful types of thinking. These shifts of body and mind will have a significant influence on your approach to co-parenting and your reactions to your other parent. Your relationship can improve in ways that you currently may think impossible. To focus on process is not to trivialize the content. Certainly, you face many consequential issues in your current situation. You must engage with those issues and work toward the wisest and most satisfying solutions. It is my hope that rather than facing those issues with little sense of control or reactive hostility, you can meet your challenges with clarity and responsibility.

## *The Ideal Co-parenting Relationship*

If you were to wave a magic wand and have the ideal co-parenting relationship, what would it look like? Perhaps, like many parents, you believe it would look like a friendship. Friends hold each other in positive regard. They are flexible when dealing with each other. There is give and take. There is closeness. Friends do enjoyable things together. In some ways, this may seem desirable. You might even know of a set of parents who co-parent like friends. But, while friendships have elements that make for good co-parenting, it is not necessary to be true friends in order to have a functional relationship as separated parents. Steering toward friendly relating is helpful. Expecting co-parenting to look exactly like friendship is setting the bar too high and may result in a feeling of failure.

So, think for a minute about what goes into a good co-parenting relationship. Clear, civil communication. Collaboration around mutual interests and goals. Respect of the other's role and individual autonomy. Trust. Certainly these exist in a friendship. But, they exist in other types of relationships as well.

Another reason I don't encourage you to model your co-parenting relationship on a friendship is that people normally behave in a friendly manner toward their friends because they *feel* friendly feelings toward and *think* friendly thoughts about that person. If we rely on this, then we will see clear, civil, collaborative, respectful, trust-building behaviors only *after* the parents start feeling and thinking this way toward each other and only in moments when they actively feel and think this way. For most children, we would wait too long for their parents to feel and think positively enough to naturally behave in a friendly manner. These qualities need to emerge in the co-parenting relationship *before* they are the result of positive feelings and thoughts. In the following chapters, I will discuss the value of steering toward less negative thoughts. I do think this is essential for constructive co-parenting. However, I do not suggest that you co-parent simply by trying to be friends.

The final reason I discourage using friendship as a model for co-parenting is that friendship often entails a level of closeness that isn't appropriate or desirable for many parents (especially in the early stage of separation). Separated parents renegotiate boundaries. After separation new boundaries exist. This is normal and desirable. Trying to be friends might undermine the project of maintaining healthy boundaries. Later, when the boundaries have been renegotiated, maintained for some time, and are serving all involved in a satisfying way, there is the possibility of becoming more like friends.

So, if the idea of friendship significantly down the line gives you a helpful ideal toward which to steer, great! By all means use it as a guidepost. But, don't set yourselves up for failure by simply seeing a functional co-parenting relationship as a friendship. Even if that is a reasonable future goal, most parents wouldn't be able to jump quickly from confusion and conflicts to being friends. Life just doesn't work that way.

For additional ideas, I recommend that you read *Mom's House Dad's House* by *Isolina Ricci*. In the middle chapters of her book, she explains a model of co-parenting based on a business relationship. She holds that two people can do business with each other, even if they don't genuinely like each other as long as there is good communication, civility, clarity of individual roles and shared projects, and written communication (which verifies agreements and transactions, such as a receipt from a store showing you what you purchased and for what price). Business relationships and transactions flow more smoothly when these things are in place.

# 2 THIS IS YOUR BRAIN ON DIVORCE

You are a physical being. And, you are wired to physically react to perceptions of danger. This stress reaction can help your body react with strength and endurance in the face of physical danger. It also has a profound effect on your brain and your perceptions. When the so-called *fight-or-flight* reaction happens, your perceptions shift dramatically. Evolutionary psychologists have explained that these shifts were beneficial in perceiving and reacting to physical dangers, such as being chased by a giant bear. However, these stress-related changes—in the body and mind—do not serve us well in situations of non-physical stress—ones in which we don't actually have to jump or run. In this chapter, I will explain the mechanics of the stress reaction and how it is relevant to post-divorce stress. I will explain how to reduce the effect of that stress in order to navigate challenging situations more effectively.

*The Physical Stress Response*

When you perceive danger, this information is quickly routed to several parts of your brain as well as glands in your endocrine system. Most of the glands of the endocrine system reside on the underside of the brain. They include the amygdala, the thalamus, the hypothalamus, and the pituitary gland. The adrenal glands reside on the tops of your kidneys. When these glands get signals from the brain, they send out stress hormones which influence the other glands to produce more hormones and influence target organs to immediately function differently. This is why your heart is beating wildly a couple of seconds after you narrowly miss getting hit by another car in traffic.

In the short-term, these physical changes can make us physically stronger and able to exhibit increased physical endurance. In the long-term, chronic stress doesn't serve us well because it contributes to cardiovascular disease, high blood pressure, and a large number of other health issues. And, it interferes with objective, positive, future-oriented perceptions.

*A Sense of Control*

It is important to have an understanding of your stress reaction. Simply knowing that you are having a stress reaction places information in your conscious mind that helps you feel more in control of your situation. Feeling out of control leads to a bigger stress reaction. So, one way to lower your overall stress level is to have less of a sense of being out of control. I'll explain with a hypothetical situation…

Imagine a sadistic psychologist conducting an experiment on two people. He puts each person alone in a room and does the same thing: he gives them a glass of soda to which he has added extra caffeine, say, the equivalent amount that would typically be in five cups of coffee. Neither person regularly drinks any sort of caffeinated beverages, so they will not have the tolerance that you would see in a regular coffee or caffeinated-soda drinker. The dose the psychologist has added will undoubtedly have a noticeable and dramatic physical effect.

In this experiment, the researcher decides to do one thing different between the two people. With the first, when giving the drink, he says, *Please drink this glass of soda, but know before you do, I have added a moderately high dose of caffeine which will likely cause some physical effects which may last for some time before wearing off.* With the second he merely says, *Please drink this glass of soda.*

Both people got the same dose of caffeine. Both will experience the same direct effects of the drug. Which one do you think will be more stressed? If you're like me, you will guess that the one who was told about the caffeine will be distressed, but not as much as the other. Both people will likely feel agitated with racing heart rates and some perceptual shifts. But, the one who knows she got the caffeine will know why she's experiencing the effects and that they will wear off. If she's concerned about it, she knows what questions to ask. She will know that her distress is limited to the effects of caffeine. But, the other person has no idea why she is experiencing these symptoms. She had no clue from the researcher about an explanation for her discomfort. She expected to feel the way she usually feels after drinking a glass of soda. When she starts feeling the caffeine symptoms, she may start thinking she's having a heart attack or going crazy—both situations much more critical than just having too much coffee.

So, the lesson here is twofold. First, when we aren't conscious of a reason to be experiencing something distressful, we feel less in control and more stressed. Knowing a reason for something will help us feel more in control even if it doesn't change the objective reality. And, when we don't know an explanation, our brain will fill in the missing data and make up an explanation. The second subject who doesn't know why she is experiencing discomfort won't ignore it. Quite the opposite. She'll focus on it and start immediately explaining it in her head, giving words to the most catastrophic fears. *I'm having a heart attack!. I'm going crazy!*

*Know that you are stressed*

This may sound like stupid advice. Of course, you know that you are stressed! But, as explained in the previous section, when you are conscious of the source of your stress, you will feel less out of control. This is important. I'm not suggesting that you focus on being stressed in ways that lead you to more stress. It is unhelpful to fret if it causes your stress level to go up or keeps you stuck in negative thinking. The goal is to get the feedback loop of your stress to calm down, not increase.

Remember the hypothetical experiment with the subjects given caffeine. Being aware of the stress reaction brings it down a notch or two because without the awareness, you feel more out of control. It is a given that you will have physical, mental, and emotional stress symptoms. What I want you to do is practice noticing them, naming them for what they are—ways that you are reacting to your current set of stressors.

I suggest you learn to do the following exercise when you are alone, and not likely to be interrupted for a few minutes: Sit comfortably in a chair or lie down. Notice your breath. Don't try to change your breathing. Just breathe and notice the parts of your body which move as you inhale and exhale. Follow your breath for a minute or two. As you relax a bit, notice your body. Do you notice tension or pain? Can you feel your heartbeat? What physical sensations are evident? Then, pay attention to your mental state. Are you alert, foggy, tired, forgetful, focused, confused, today? What other aspects of your mental state do you notice? What words would you use to describe your attitude, today? Also, take some time to name your emotional state. Is your emotional energy stable or mixed, today? What emotion words would you use to name your emotional reactions, today? End by going back to your breath for another minute.

This strategy is beneficial because it helps you frame your stress as: *I am experiencing stress and I am reacting to it*. Again, not a profound insight. But, it is replacing the alternative and very unhelpful inner explanation: *My ex is making my life hell!* There is a subtle, but very powerful difference between those two ways of framing your experience of stress. The one I am suggesting (*I am experiencing stress…*) implies that you are the one aware of your stress. You are the one reacting in a particular manner. If you don't like the reaction, you are potentially in control of changing it. The second, and common, way of framing it (*My ex…*) reduces your sense of control in the situation. If I think, *You make me so mad!*, then you are the one in control of my emotions. What can I do about it then except try to control you or escape you.

When I work with parents, I hear this type of blaming language all the time. And, I believe speaking that way starts by thinking that way. Some parts of our experience are out of our control. But, much is within our control. We need to know the difference. We rob ourselves of opportunities to take responsibility when we think that we are out of control when we really aren't. And, when we maintain that out-of-control frame of reference, we only increase our overall stress level. Make this shift in your thinking so that you are not ignoring your stress, then only attributing it to your ex when it becomes so strong you can't ignore it.

The strategy also helps by being specific. We all have a relatively accurate intuitive, but vague, sense of how stressed we are. If I were to ask you to rate your current stress level on a scale of one to ten, you won't have to think long before deciding on where you rank. However, that vague sense is too easily attributed to things out of our control and it doesn't help us focus on our stress reaction in ways that make it more likely that we can do something about it. For example, if I were to say, "*Yesterday I was upset, so I didn't sleep well,*" or, "*Today I'm noticing that I'm more clumsy,*" then I know a bit more about what I can do to counteract the negative effects of my stress—try to get better sleep tonight and pay extra careful attention when doing something important like driving a car.

*Generally lower your stress level*

Most of the unhelpful brain effects described in this chapter increase as stress increases. It doesn't matter what the sources are and it doesn't matter why you are at your current stress level. What matters is that you are currently registering an ongoing stress level that is probably above normal for your life in general. And, during this prolonged period of stress, you will have many moments when that stress level will spike to an even higher point. I encourage you to do two things.

First, you should do things that generally lower your stress. This will be helpful even if they aren't focused on specifically dealing with post-separation issues. If you are dealing with your stress—through yoga, a hobby, exercise, or something else—then when you have your spikes, they start from a lower point. You will also become more skilled at coming down from a spike. And, you can keep more of your frontal lobe online more of the time. I also recommend doing what you can to get good sleep. Poor sleep is a pervasive and chronic issue in our society. And, poor sleep increases your stress response.

Second, I want you to learn some specific short (one to five minute) techniques to help you lower your stress level in situations when you are triggered and have to deal with your ex or your children. This will help you have more of a sense of control because you will be consciously choosing to do something rather than waiting for your ex to do something to you. And, even if it doesn't prevent a spike in your stress level, you can keep from getting as strongly stressed if you have prepared by calming down ahead of time. If you only go to *Code Yellow* instead of *Code Orange* during an encounter with your ex, then you will keep more of your frontal lobe online and will more likely keep pointed in a positive direction.

You will find in chapter nine several stress reduction techniques. All are useful if performed regularly to lower your overall stress level and retrain your brain to unhook from stress. Some are useful as preparatory activities right before you encounter an expected stressful situation. Practicing stress management techniques, even for a few minutes each day, will provide a cumulative effect, too. Over time, the parts of your brain which counteract these negative effects described in this book will be strengthened. Your frontal lobe will not only stay online more of the time, but, will be better able to function the way you need it to. The techniques are simple, but you must persevere to get the maximum effect. If you try stress management techniques but are underwhelmed by the immediate effect, it might be because you're under a lot of stress, not that you performed the technique wrong or that it isn't working.

## The Negative Lens through Which You View the Other Parent

If you are not conscious of the stress reaction, you will feel more out of control and more stressed which will magnify the stress response—an unhelpful cycle. And, being less conscious of what is happening, your big brain will fill in the missing data—usually with some version of: *This is all hell. My ex is evil, stupid, and crazy!*

The problem is then compounded because after your brain makes up an explanation, it is also wired to look for data that confirms it. The subject who believes she is having a heart attack will confirm that belief by noticing and focusing on her heart rate. Hundreds of parents have spent a lot of effort trying to convince me that co-parenting can't work because their ex really is evil, stupid, and crazy and they are out of control to do anything about it. This is largely because they are attributing much of their stress reaction to the other parent. It's the most likely explanation their brain can provide of why they are feeling as stressed as they are.

## Losing Perspective

Another aspect of how stress influences brain activity relevant to these situations is that under stress, some parts of our brain shut down. And, unfortunately, the main part that shuts down is one you need. There's a technical term for this: *reciprocal inhibition*. In this case, when the stress parts of your brain light up, the frontal lobe tends to shut down. To understand why this is a problem, let's discuss the role of the frontal lobe.

Your frontal lobe (and mine and everybody else's) is the part of your brain that allows you to think positively, creatively, and about the future. In technical terms, this is sometimes called *proception*. It is the ability to imagine a reality that is not directly happening to you to the extent that you can evaluate it or react to it.

Imagine that I were to give you three thousand dollars to take a weekend vacation to the destination of your choice. Where you would go? What you would do? If you were asked this question while under a functional magnetic resonance imaging machine (fMRI), we would see the frontal lobe light up while you were thinking about sitting on the beach in Cancun sipping a smoothie. It is also the part that allows you to do crucial things like imagine what other people are feeling, to have empathy. It helps us have perspective, to not only live in the present, but to have a wider view of our experience both to avoid future realities which we won't like, and to steer toward those we think we will. You would use this part of your brain if you were talking to someone about something you were trying to convince them to do for you say, loan you their car for the weekend, in order to track their cognitive state to your advantage. It's also why you don't have to pour BBQ sauce on your ice cream to decide whether it will make the dessert more tasty. You use this part of your brain to imagine that future, and avoid it.

So, when stress goes up, the frontal lobe shuts down. And, from an evolutionary standpoint, this makes sense. Our ancestors weren't wired to think about where they wanted to live in retirement while fighting a saber tooth tiger. They survived because their brains—now ours—were wired to focus powerfully on the present danger.

This is, again, a twofold problem for separated parents who need to deal with each other positively and creatively to be civil and negotiate solutions to the complexities of co-parenting *and* stay future-oriented to maintain a good working relationship into the future. I see this effect sabotage my clients often. Let me give you a recent example to illustrate…

A set of parents was in my office swearing that they fight about everything and agree on nothing. They were hopeless about co-parenting. They shared a nine-year old daughter and, by their account, she was healthy, happy, and doing relatively fine. I assumed that a thriving, well-adjusted child must have parents who cooperate—at least part of the time—on how to best nurture her. They couldn't really mean that they fight about *everything*! I asked them to name something they *didn't* fight about.

But, when I asked this question, they drew a blank. They really couldn't think of a single thing that they didn't fight about. So, I gave them an answer. Earlier in the same initial session, they had told me that they: 1) were both Christians, 2) were Baptist, 3) wanted to raise their daughter as a Baptist, 4) had been sending her to a private Christian school for two years, 5) had been splitting the tuition for the school and, 6) both did parent volunteer hours each week as required by the school. I pointed this out and asked, *When was the last time you had a fight about any of those six things?* They were silent. They admitted that, actually, they were in agreement about all of those—they hadn't even ever fought over the ratio of splitting the tuition. But, when I asked about what was positive and working for their daughter's future…things contributing to a positive co-parenting relationship, they couldn't access any of it.

They were sincere in telling me that they only saw negative data when looking at the other parent. They weren't lying to me. But, they were *wrong*! And, they were seeing it that way because they were stressed about their unresolved conflicts and their frontal lobes were shut down. They had lost perspective.

Now, don't get me wrong here. I'm in no way suggesting that the issues these parents faced were trivial. My wanting them to see the positive was not to try to get them to merely see a rosy picture of their situation. But, I noticed that they had lost sight of the positive. And, that was not serving them well. It was contributing to their spiraling into more and more conflict. If you can't see half of the data, if you are not perceiving the positive, then those positive things aren't as fully *in-play* as they could be. I call this *missing the green slice*.

Imagine a pie chart…a big circle. And, imagine that red is the color for *divorce hell*. Green is the color of *the good stuff*. If I asked these parents to make a pie chart for their co-parenting relationship, they would probably draw a circle that was all red with no green slice.

That's what they were telling me, there is nothing positive, we fight about everything. But, it simply wasn't true!

You'll probably agree with me that people in the early stages of a relationship are often wearing rose-colored glasses. They aren't seeing REALITY. We call this the *honeymoon effect*. However, people after divorce are, for months or years, wearing crap-colored glasses when they look at each other. Your other parent could do something golden and you wouldn't even see it. And you might try to convince me that you are seeing REALITY. And, you would be wrong!

*Be Conscious of the Green Slice to Keep Positivity in Play!*

Over the last fifteen years, hundreds of parents have shown me their strengths and successes as co-parents (through their behaviors and giving me their histories) and then, moments later, sworn that the green slice doesn't exist. This is a huge problem when you very much need the green slice and you need to be consciously aware of it. If you look over at your other parent and only see all red for your pie chart, that is a truly very hellish situation. And, being so utterly hellish, your brain will use it to fire off an *even bigger* stress reaction which compounds the problem.

The other reason this is a problem is in the effect it has on your behavior. If you think the other parent is *all bad all of the time*, you will react as though it's true. You will tend to have only negative reactions…few neutral and little or no positive. Your negative reactions will provide proof to the other parent that their negative thinking about you is true and the cycle is compounded. You two spiral into an increasingly negative pattern.

In the example I just described, imagine if one of these parents did see the green slice. Imagine if one had said to the other something like, *Look, I know we fight about a lot of things and probably need to work on being more civil with each other for the sake of our daughter. But, I want you to know that I am grateful that we both want to raise our daughter as a Christian. I'm grateful that we both value that enough to send her to a Christian school and share the tuition without fighting about it.*

Saying that would have only taken about forty seconds and would have burned nearly zero calories. And, it would have reinforced the green slice. But, they will never say that as long as they truly believe that there is no green slice. Instead, they will only focus on the things they fight about. They will only react to the other person as an adversary, somebody who not only fights with them, but fights with them about the person they care about most. This brain effect can steer parents into lasting conflict. All because our ancestors were wired to not stop and smell the roses while being chased by a giant bear!

*Create the Green Slice*

One way to examine this is to do the following two tasks: Right now, I want you to think of three things you dislike about the other parent or three things that don't work between you—as coparents. Now I want you to think of three things you appreciate about the other parent or three things that you two do well together as separated coparents. Which task took more time? Were you able to name five negative *and* five positive things? Many parents can't name *any* positive things, or come up with something not so useful like, *Well, I don't think my ex has ever murdered someone.* (A parent actually said that when I posed this question one time.)

The good parts are there. But, when you are unconscious of them, they are not fully in play. If you are unable to even think of something positive, you will not communicate it to the other parent. You will be less likely to behave in a way that optimally expresses that strength. You will continue to behave in an overly negative manner. This will slow your progress toward a more workable co-parenting relationship.

Another reason to become conscious of the green slice is to have more *objective* perspective about the other parent. Only seeing the bad parts and remaining fairly unconscious of any good parts translates into a hellish state of mind. You look across at the other parent and only see bad things. However accurate your perceptions are of the other parents faults, ignoring the green slice means you are having a skewed perception of them in the negative direction. This will result in even more stress for you which compounds the process. It also means you begin interactions with them already more triggered than you should be. It contributes to the risk of spiraling into an unsatisfying argument.

Identifying the green slice is one of the more difficult things you need to do as a separated parent. And, you should do it because it is so very, very valuable. It is essential to unhook from some of your negative thinking in order to have more objectivity and craft a more positive relationship. Know that your brain will be running interference for you when you try to look for the green slice. Here's an example from a parent with whom I talked recently. A separated father was speaking with me, angrily, about his ex-wife. He said he thought she "didn't care at all about" their children. When I asked why he thought that, he told me that when he dropped his children off for their most recent weekend parenting time with their mother, he asked her to spend some time working on the son's homework which was due Monday morning. He picked the children up on Sunday afternoon and, after returning home, discovered that the son had not finished any of his homework. The dad proceeded to punish the son by taking the daughter out to dinner and making the son stay home and work on homework. He then called the mother in front of the children to tell her she sucked and should have done the homework with the son and that it was her fault the son was upset about not getting to join the dad and sister for dinner. This is a father stuck in divorce hell and unable to see the green slice.

Now, I do agree that parents should generally support their children in completing homework. The father had a reasonable expectation for the mother and communicated it clearly when he dropped of the children at the beginning of the weekend. It is understandable that he was annoyed at the mother for not doing the homework during the weekend, or at least some of it. However, the father provided only that one bit of evidence for his strong conviction that his ex-wife was evil, stupid, and crazy, and a bad mother. He mentioned no way in which the mother failed to parent the daughter. And, the homework was the only issue with the son. Assuming the children were with the mother from Friday evening to Sunday afternoon, that is a lot of parenting time. I assume that, if we had a video of all the interactions between the mother and the children during that time, we would see her making a lot of parenting decisions. Every time our children are with us, we make dozens of parenting decisions. We don't always succeed in keeping our children happy in every moment. But, we keep them alive and healthy. We nurture them. We contribute to their overall wellbeing. We maintain and develop our relationships with them. I had no direct evidence of the ex-wife's mothering. But, in the absence of more damning evidence other than not having helped complete the son's homework, I'm going to assume she was doing many things that were neutral to positive related to the children's needs.

So, part of the lesson here is that you will ignore the green slice because you believe your complaints are legitimate. The father thought (and I agreed) that the request for the mother to help with the homework was reasonable. However, when she didn't do as he expected, he only focused on that issue and completely excluded all other aspects of her mothering of their shared children. Surely, there are consequential or triggering issues and I'm not suggesting you see them as trivial. Perhaps this son is not doing well in school and it is crucial for both parents to be on top of his homework. Perhaps the father does need to discuss how the mother and he can best support the son in doing well in school. But, the father must also see the mother more objectively and not represented only by her failure to comply with his request that weekend around the homework.

*Step One*: Notice that you will sometimes do this exclusionary thinking. You will focus only on the triggering issue and lose sight of the positive aspects of the situation. *Step Two*: Identify additional positive aspects in your situation. This is also tricky. I know this because I have had many parents sit in my office staring blankly at me when I ask them to name something that is positive about the other parent or their co-parenting relationship. It is out of their awareness and not available for immediate recall. They have a blind spot. Some things out of our conscious awareness are really there, but you just have to expend some effort and shift your attention to get the information.

Perhaps you haven't focused strongly on the weather over the past two days consciously. But, if I were to ask you if it has rained, you could tell me. You have the information, but weren't thinking of it until I asked. But, if there is information that you simply aren't tracking, then it won't be available even if you try to access it. If I ask you to tell me about the quality of your breath over the last five minutes while you have been reading this book, you probably won't be able to tell me very much (unless, maybe, you have a cold or some reason you have been focused on your breathing). You might assume you have been breathing because you are alive but, that isn't much detail about how your actual breathing has been going. You could only tell me more about your breath if you placed your attention on it. So, you will only be able to be conscious of the green slice if you choose to pay attention to it. Perhaps with some careful thinking, you can come up with something. That is good. I celebrate that, if you can. If you can't, then you need to consciously choose to notice this information and do that often.

Developing a co-parenting plan helps in creating the green slice. A co-parenting plan is a document that spells out individual values or agreements related to your situation. The types of issues (custody and parenting time schedules) included in court orders or mediated agreements are relevant to co-parenting plans. But, such plans need to include a wider range of issues than those included in the litigation process. How you will divide Little League fees might be relevant to your co-parenting plan, but trivial in terms of your court process. As you have conversations about co-parenting issues and come to agreements, write them down. Share them back and forth in e-mails. This growing document is evidence of the things that you are *not* fighting about. Most parents don't create such a document, but should. If they did, then they wouldn't be so confused when I ask about the things around which they have agreement. See Isolina Ricci's book, *Mom's House Dad's House*, for additional advice about developing a co-parenting plan, or search for samples online.

Another very useful tool is the online resource UpToParents.org. I recommend going to this free site and using it to identify the green slice. The site has a couple of useful functions. One is to list many specific ideas that parents often value about co-parenting. You can choose those which you value and those you don't. In this way, you will identify some specific, positive ideas about co-parenting to use to build your co-parenting relationship. This is better than negative, reactive co-parenting.

The process of sorting through the co-parenting ideas on the site can be very helpful in identifying not only what you might want to pursue in your co-parenting future, but what already actually exists. The other function of the site is to merge your answers with those of the other parent (if you both do the site) and give you a report on what you are saying you agree. I think this shared report can be a good tool for having an ongoing conversation about building a workable co-parenting relationship. But, it can also help identify the green slice. For example, if both you and the other parent say that you agree that you support your child having a positive relationship with the other parent (one of the ideas on the site the last time I looked), then it may lead to thinking about how you each can do that. Certainly your big brains, swirling through high stress and focused on lots of unresolved conflict, can quickly come up with the ways the other parent fails to do that. But, if you are honest with yourself, you can also see ways that the other parent does support your relationship with your child. I do recommend you go use that site, even if your other parent doesn't. It is useful for shifting your thinking from the negative, reactive mode to focus on specific, positive ideas related to co-parenting.

An alternative to using the web site is getting out a notebook and spending some time contemplating the green slice. At first, you may sit and stare at the paper unable to think of anything. But, it is there. You just aren't seeing it. This may be challenging to do. But, it is important. One way I try to help parents identify the positive parts they are missing is to think of how things could be worse. Recently, a father told me how awful his ex-wife was because she took their daughter to the doctor without telling him. The mom did call the dad after the appointment, but the dad had wanted to know before such appointments. Again, the dad is having a reasonable desire. But, his focus on the mother's failure to comply with their general agreement to do that in that situation causes him to miss other important parts. Here's how I was thinking about the situation.

The daughter, age 13, one morning at the mother's house complained of sharp pain when she peed. The daughter was shy about discussing this type of thing with the father, but was fairly open with the mother. So, the mother sent the daughter to school, made an appointment with the doctor, later picked her up from school, and took the daughter to see the doctor where she was diagnosed with a yeast infection. The mother then went to the pharmacy to get some medicine and took the daughter back to school. Then the mother called the father to inform him of what had transpired. At this point, the parents got into an argument that resulted in each of them threatening to take the other one to court for a change of custody. Let's think about all the things that went right in that situation.

The daughter was sick and needed to go to the doctor. She has a close relationship with her mom and told her mom quickly that she was having discomfort. The mother immediately called to make an appointment that day and sent the daughter to school to wait for the doctor's office to schedule the appointment. Because the mom sent the daughter to school, less school work was missed. The mom personally picked the daughter up from school. She didn't have some other person do this. The mom accompanied the daughter to the doctor's office. Then the mom got the medicine and delivered the daughter back to school so she could finish the school day. The mom then called the dad. The daughter was able to quickly get medical attention while with someone she trusted and also not miss too much school. And, the father completely ignored all of this because he focused on being angry with the mom for not calling him sooner about the medical issue.

If the father can think of nothing good, then it couldn't be worse, right? From his perspective, the mom is all bad and there is no good to her parenting. So, he ignored that it would have been worse if the mom ignored the daughter's pain. He ignored that the mom has a close relationship with the daughter that makes it possible for them to discuss sensitive health issues. He ignored that the daughter was supported in being in school as much as possible that day, even while having to go to the appointment. He ignored that the daughter was with someone whom she knows and trusts. From the father's perspective, it is all bad and there is no good. There are many ways that situation could have been worse. But, it wasn't. And, the father wasn't aware of it because of his exclusive focus on the one aspect.

Get skilled at noticing when your brain does this very thing. It will. You are a normal person who is wired to not see the green slice. But, it is there. Every case I have worked in, even the worst ones, had positive parts and the parents were usually totally missing them. Consequently, these positive parts are not fully in play. And, because the parents miss them, they spiral into unnecessary and damaging conflict. Use the green slice to your advantage to steer out of that negativity. The goal is not to make you genuinely like the other parent. It is possible that will never happen. And, the goal is not to trivialize important issues. I support you in identifying important issues and working for collaboration around them. In the example with the daughter, these parents do need to clarify their policy around medical appointments. But, they each need to be able to put their difficulties in perspective along with the good parts. Miss the green slice and you are working at a disadvantage.

*Fast and Slow Thinking*

The stress-related parts of our brains have evolved to act quickly. Some of the non-stress parts function more slowly. Again, from an evolutionary standpoint, this makes sense. It is helpful for us to notice something snake-like in our peripheral vision and jump out of the way even before we consciously take the time to think, *Wait, that looked like a snake...maybe I should consider jumping out of the way!*

You have fast and slow aspects to your brain. Let me give you an example. If I ask you what three times six is, you probably don't have to think very long before you have the answer: eighteen. You got this quickly because you spent so long in elementary school memorizing the multiplication tables. It's like a groove in your brain. But, if I ask what is half of three times seven, you will have to access the slow part of your brain before you come up with the answer: ten point five. This fast part of our brain serves us well in many situations. After you learn to ride a bicycle, you can use the fast part to govern your muscle movements to push and steer the bicycle while you enjoy a safe ride through the park enjoying the scenery.

The stress part is mainly in the fast category. But in stressful situations, this can work against us. If there really is a snake on the forest path or a rock in the road to avoid, the fast part will keep us safe. But, in many situations when we need to access the slow, deliberative part of our brain—which is partly shut down due to high stress—we may react as though there is greater danger than there really is. And, as I said before, we will react without thought for the future. Let me explain…

*Know When the Building Is On fire and When It Isn't*

One way our brains help us survive is to assess *importance* and *urgency*. Importance has to do with how big the consequences are. Urgency has to do with whether the consequences will get bigger over time. We need this function to survive. If the building is on fire, we need our brains to perceive this as both important *and* urgent! As you might guess, our brains are wired to err on the side of thinking that issues are more important and urgent than they really are. To make the opposite mistake would have killed our ancestors, so we're wired to make this type of misjudgment. Those individuals hanging out with our ancestors who chilled out too much in the face of danger all got eaten by giant bears and didn't produce offspring to become us. So, we inherit this function of quickly over-reacting to potential danger. But, as separated co-parents, it doesn't always serve us well.

If we always made slow, deliberative judgments about how important and urgent an issue was, we would sometimes react quickly and, most of the time, react slowly, or not at all. In reality, the building usually isn't on fire. But, when we get triggered by our ex, we often react immediately and with great force, as though we were about to be bitten by a saber tooth tiger. It could be about anything. *The $100 copay for the dental bill is due next month. I think we should send only one, not two, cookies with Mary's lunch at daycare. I think bedtime should be 9:00 instead of 9:30 on school nights.* Before stopping to take a second to assess how important and urgent the issue is, a parent is quick to jump into an argument about it.

I see this frequently in mediation. By the time parents get to the first session of mediation, their big brains have thought of many issues, and they believe they are all ultra important and very urgent! They want to argue over everything and act as though the building is on fire. But, from where I'm sitting, many of the issues seem best left out of the mediation and, if important at all, better served as part of a co-parenting plan (a co-parenting plan spells out parenting agreements, but includes a wide range of issues, not just the big ones that are often part of litigation or mediation). They're not crazy— though the other parent will swear they are. They're just stressed out and their brains are making things seem more important and urgent than they really are.

Remember I explained that , when stressed, your brain is wired to view issues as more important and more urgent than they actually are.

This is due to the fight-or-flight response. Evolution has shaped our brains to quickly focus on and magnifying potentially dangerous situations. For millions of years, it was helpful for our ancestors to over-react to mildly dangerous situations. Survival depended on it. Having the opposite tendency—to under-react to potentially dangerous situations—would have killed off our ancestors. But, this tendency does not always serve us well. In the situation of co-parenting after separation, it is a particularly unhelpful effect.

Certainly, you are dealing with many important issues. And, many of them are urgent, needing to be addressed sooner rather than later. I am not suggesting that you pretend that everything is trivial and can be put off. But, when I work with parents, I notice that many of their interactions were about relatively unimportant issues which could have been avoided, or not emphasized so strongly. And, many times they react with great urgency when they could have delayed focusing on the issue or put it off until they were able to deal with it more effectively. You are going to be better off if you learn to sort issues into low- to high-importance and low- to high-urgency. But your brain is going to run interference for you. Here's what I suggest you do about it.

First, just knowing that you have this tendency will be helpful. You won't correct for it if you don't notice that it exists. You could probably tell me that there have been several interactions with your other parent when you realized (after it was all over) that you could have just not dealt with it at all, or could have put it off until later. I'm guessing you can think of several instances when you, or the other parent, over-reacted because you were triggered and acted as though an issue was urgent and of great importance. This may be easier to see in the other parent. But, I bet you do this, too. To put this into practice, actually think of the last few interactions in which you initiated communication with your other parent. Write them down on a sheet of paper. Give each issue a score from zero to ten for relative importance from your *current* perspective, not how you were viewing it at the time. Notice if there were any that were of relatively low importance, but which you treated as highly important when you actually communicated about them. Also, note if each one was urgent or not. Remember that urgency is different from importance. An urgent issue is one which needs to be addressed sooner, rather than later. And, by needing to be addressed sooner, I'm meaning some factor other than, *I just want this solved right now because it's bugging me*. The fact that you have a sense of urgency around an issue doesn't make it urgent. And, for issues which have some aspect of urgency (for example a deadline coming up for registering a child for summer camp), often parents are trying to solve the issue long before it actually needs to be addressed. Urgency is magnified just like importance.

Many issues during, and after, separation are important and some are urgent. This is especially true close to the time when parents are actually separating. There are many issues which have to do with money, property, and children which need to be addressed. Your big brain is working overtime focusing on dozens of these issues. One strategy I recommend is keeping a notebook in which you can write issues as they pop into your head. This is a brainstorming exercise because it is intended to allow you to think about a wide set of issues without trying to edit them in your head before you write them down. Feel free to write anything you think of in this notebook. If you construct a list of issues in your notebook this way, rank them by relative importance. You can either do this by sorting them into high, mid-range, and low importance. Or, you can give them an importance score of zero to ten.

After you rank your issues by importance, then mark them urgent or not. If they have no deadline, or can be decided later with little additional consequence, then they are non-urgent. If they have a time factor (for example, we need to determine the amount of equity in the house prior to our first scheduled mediation session three weeks from now), then write the specific date before which action is required. Write the specific actions required around that issue so you know what steps need to be taken and when.

After sorting importance, you can use this information to choose whether or not to attempt to address the issue with your other parent. Some issues of low importance are probably best left off the agenda altogether. And, some issues of low or moderate importance might better be dealt with as they seem prudent, or in the right circumstances. For example, when I am mediating a divorce, sometimes parents bring up issues that have some importance, but not for the mediation process. They might be better served as issues included in a co-parenting plan outside the mediation. They are not issues which need to be spelled out in a mediated agreement and written into a divorce decree. A co-parenting plan is an informal document between parents about issues and agreements that isn't necessarily entered into litigation or written formally as a mediated agreement. An example of something that parents might include in a co-parenting plan would be an agreement that one parent be generally responsible for taking a child to a sports practice. It may have some importance and the parents are well served to be clear about their agreement. But, it isn't necessary to spell this out in a divorce decree which could result in loss of flexibility later or, worse, something over which they might fight in court.

For issues that have some urgency, it is good to be aware of the specific time factor for the urgency. If you know that you have three weeks to make a decision about an issue, that is a different situation from needing to decide by tomorrow. Again, if you don't get clear about this, your brain will make things more urgent than they really are. And, if you aren't clear, then your vague sense of urgency will make all of the issues of immediate importance. Your stressed-out brain is wired to tell you the building is on fire! Often, it isn't.

Another benefit of sorting issues this way is that you can choose which ones you emphasize and also how you deal with them. If live communication doesn't always work well for you and other parent, then you can deal with the more urgent and important issues live and leave the less urgent and less important ones for e-mail or text conversations. In the previous section of this chapter, I discussed the benefits of going non-live in communication. Sorting issues by importance and urgency can help you decide which ones to deal with in which ways. I suggest Mark Goulston's book, *Just Listen: Discover the Secret to Getting Through to Absolutely Anyone* for an accessible, rich discussion of the importance of calming the fast part of your brain during interpersonal conflict.

## *My Ex is Evil, Stupid, and Crazy!*

Another post-separation pitfall parents face is the effect grief has on the brain. Divorce triggers, on average, the biggest grief reaction people ever face. When studies rank all life events from low to high stress, divorce makes the top of the list. This is because divorce is not one thing, but many to which we react. Consider this: if you weren't divorcing, but you took a new job in a different location which required you to sell your house and move, the stress of moving would be pretty high. Moving entails many details and adjustments for you and your family, even if for a good reason. But, however stressful moving is, in a divorce it is often just one part of a big basket of stressful adjustments. And, they take place all in a fairly short period of time and then last for months or years. This is why divorce ranks the highest on the stress list and why it is such a big grief trigger.

From the onset of the separation, sometimes even before, your brain is reacting to several big adjustments. Your identity changes. You might move to a new residence. Your income and debt profile may change. Your time with your children may change. So many things. Each one would be stressful alone. But, altogether, they add up to a huge level of stress along with strong emotional reactions. These are influencing your brain just like the other effects I have explained. Here's how I tend to see the effect of the grief reaction after separation in my clients.

During the period of adjustment and grief after separation, parents tend to be stuck in a negative thinking/feeling mode. This is normal. People do this during and after a break-up. You wake up every day feeling miserable and can't *not* think about worries and disappointments related to your situation. You may also be, for some time, in a limbo state, not knowing if it's really happening, if divorce will be the final outcome. You may still be invested in the relationship, fighting to save it and up against the other partner who seems to have bailed. And, again, there is no "off" button for this negative mental state. Pleasurable distractions tend to only work for short periods and many people turn to drinking or other means to try to unhook from it. (But, those strategies generally have risks and costs and don't really solve the issue. I discourage them.) Tomorrow, you wake up and are in the exact same state.

Here's the non-clinical way I describe this negative state driven by this lasting grief reaction. Because your brain is so focused on the negative thoughts and feelings of the experience, they crowd out non-divorce information. They take up the whole screen. Your brain, being so focused on this one situation, will relate all non-divorce information through the divorce lens. I see the process like this...Random input is processed through the lens of:

> **This is all Hell because my ex is Evil, Stupid, and Crazy...and let me tell you about it!**

A father I worked with recently provides a good example of this thinking. He was at the mall with his twelve-year old daughter buying shoes for a school sport. While shopping, she saw a pair of jeans she wanted and asked him to buy them. His brain immediately went through that process—This is all Hell because my ex is Evil, Stupid and Crazy...and let me tell you about it!—and he said to her, *Well, if your mom wouldn't have had all those affairs and I wasn't now paying her attorney fees to fight me in court, I'd buy you the jeans. It's really her problem, so talk to her about it when you see her this weekend.*

The request from the daughter to buy the jeans had nothing to do with the divorce. It would have been easy to respond to her without mentioning the divorce and his anger at her mother. But, while I think he was dysfunctional for *saying* that to his daughter, I don't think he is crazy for *thinking* it. This is normal brain activity after separation. If you are not conscious of the effect, negative things about the other parent will flow smoothly out of your mouth. And, your brain will look for data that justifies those thoughts and actions. When I challenged this father about this type of behavior, he—not surprisingly—said to me, *Jon, you can't tell me to not say that because it's true!*

My response to him, and to you, is that it doesn't matter if it's "true" for you in that moment. It is happening in your head that way because of stress and grief and it leads to speech and behavior that doesn't support good parenting or good co-parenting. Be aware of this effect and steer out of it.

*Ghosts or Artifacts from the Past*

The last brain issue that I'll cover in this chapter is an effect of memory. In short, you carry along what I'll call *ghosts* or *artifacts* of your past conflicts, especially those that remain unresolved. And, these artifacts will cloud your perceptions of current reality even if the current reality is radically different from the past. This is due to the (often long) period defined as negative intimacy.

> Positive intimacy (high involvement with a net positive experiential value) came at the beginning of your relationship. However long it lasted, it eventually turned into negative intimacy (high involvement with a net negative experiential value). Since you are likely still pretty highly involved due to sharing children, I'll assume that for most readers, this period extends up until the present. Negative memories and associations come along, having been created during the negative intimacy phase. And, they reappear as artifacts, *even when something very different is happening.*

Let me explain with an example. Recently, I was working with two separated parents. They came to me for support in becoming more clear and civil communicators with each other. I taught them some of the communication skills you'll encounter later in this book and I thought they were both doing a remarkable job of putting the skills into practice. During the fifth session, something interesting happened.

In that session, the ex-husband calmly and clearly said to the ex-wife, *Next week, I think my boss will ask me to work some overtime. We might need to talk about the parenting time schedule to see if we need to shift it around a little.* While he was saying this, I noticed the ex-wife becoming noticeably very tense. I knew something interesting was going on since I had just witnessed the husband being respectful and calm. It wasn't obvious to me why she should react so strongly. I asked her what she had heard her ex-husband say and she said (with strong agitation and anger), *He said I'm a bad parent!*

Now, my guess was that the ex-husband's brain instantly chalked this up as more evidence that his ex-wife really was as stupid and crazy as he had tried to convince me at the beginning of the sessions. In fact, I saw his eyes roll which I interpreted as him having just that type of thought. He knew that he had spoken to her respectfully and had said nothing like the critical message that she reported hearing. And, he knew that I saw the same thing, so he probably was thinking that he instantly won points with me against her.

However, I have learned to watch for these artifacts. And, in fact, this set of parents had described this particular artifact, so I wasn't surprised to see it pop up. I knew from their history they gave in the intake session that one of their past, and longstanding, issues was this very thing. During their marriage and after their separation, the husband had told her in many ways that she was a bad parent. Through repetitive, emotionally powerful experiences, we program ourselves to see a certain version of reality and will continue to see it, even when the objective reality is different.

You must expect this to happen. It will be easier to see in the other parent when she or he reacts as though you did something you did *in the past*, but didn't do *just now*. This effect tends to be persistent, sticking around longer than would be helpful and popping up again at random later times. And, the outcome of this effect is that, even when parents start changing their patterns for the better, their *new* patterns will seem to have the same effect as the *old* style of conflict. This is a big reason that parents often given up hope for improvement. They tried to clean up their interactions. But, they couldn't see things getting better because of this clouding of their perception. So, they decided either they were doing it wrong, or their ex really was evil, stupid, and crazy. Don't give up too soon.

*Losing Sight of Innocent Bystanders*

When we get triggered with stress, we lose sight of peripheral information. At any given moment, we are tracking a lot of information. Some things are at the center of our awareness. Some things are nearer the edges. We often focus on the central stuff at the expense of less relevant information. This is a good thing. You wouldn't be able to drive at high speed safely down the highway if you didn't focus on the central information (driving the car) at the expense of peripheral issues (Oh, that's a pretty farmhouse, but I didn't get a very good look).

However, this can cause parents to expose children to too much conflict. It is my opinion that parents should not engage in conflict at transitions, when exchanging children. I will explain more about this later in the book. But, exchanges must be neutral, or positive, events for your children. You also should not engage in conflict when your children are present, say at the other end of the house or upstairs "sleeping." You should not be on the phone arguing with the other parent in earshot of your children. But, even parents who agree with me about this and try to avoid children witnessing their conflicts often do so anyway. This happens because they get triggered and their stressed brains lose sight of peripheral information—that the kids are aware of the conflict.

A research study recently that showed this effect. The researchers included in the study families who were going through divorce. They gave the children logs and asked them to record the day and time of any conflict between their parents. They gave the parents a log to record their conflicts and asked them to add one extra bit of information. If the parents recorded conflict in their log, they also recorded whether or not the children had any awareness that the conflict took place.

The parents in the study reported, on average, that their children were aware of 42% of their conflicts. But, their children reported that they were aware of 72% of their parents' conflicts. This is not a surprising result. And, it means that typical parents are often unaware of how their children are exposed to their conflict. When your children are present, only engage in communication with your other parent if you are certain neither of you will get triggered. Children get stressed when their parents fight, even if the fight is a relatively low-level conflict. So much separation stress is out of your control. But, some of it is directly under your control and this is one. You can take this part of separation stress off your child's plate.

I know that some of you are thinking, Yeah, right, but the other parent won't play fair and will bring up issues at transitions. I say: When the ball comes over the net, you have the choice about whether to whack it back across. Refuse to play the game. Create another forum for communication so that issues aren't funneled into the transitions or situations when your children can be, even peripherally, aware of them.

*Question Reality*

Earlier I explained that when our brain lacks information, it will fill in the gaps. And, when our brain focuses on an explanation, it will look for evidence that supports it. Separated parents are no more seeing reality than they were way back during the honeymoon phase. This phase is no different except that the early one led to a pleasurable experience and this one leads in the opposite direction.

I know when I make this assertion, your brain is likely already arguing with me. *No, Jon, I **AM** seeing reality! My ex really is a jerk!* I assume this because when I bring it up to my clients, 99% of the time, that is their reaction. Have you ever tried to convince a friend who is experiencing the honeymoon effect that their new love may not be as rosy as they think? Their eyes will glaze over and they won't be able to hear you. And, as a parent who is chronically stressed and mired in a huge mess of unresolved conflicts, you also might have trouble believing me when I say: You are not seeing *Reality*!

Remember the story of the hypothetical subject unaware that she was dosed with a moderately high amount of caffeine? She would have been likely to start thinking she was having a heart attack and supporting that belief with the evidence that her heart was racing, seemingly out of control. And, remember the parents who sat in my office and swore that they couldn't agree on anything just minutes after describing six very important things on which they agreed? The bottom line is that we are often very wrong about our assumptions, even about our ex.

When under stress, we all operate with lenses that obscure the positive and magnify the negative. During high stress, we often won't be seeing reality—even when we think we are. This is hard for us to see in ourselves, since we are operating through these lenses. It is easier to see in others which is how I became so strongly convinced of this effect. I see it over and over in the parents with whom I work. And, I can see it because I'm the third party. They operate with their individual versions of reality. But, from my vantage point, I get to see another view. I can see their creativity, positivity, and strengths even when they can't seem to.

If you remember my explaining the issue of artifacts, you'll be well-served to look for this effect. It will be easier to see in the other parent when you behave quite saintly and they respond as though you're the devil. It is much harder to see in yourself, how you will sometimes react as though your ex did something in the former, dysfunctional pattern even if that's not really what they just did.

Remember the example of the ex-wife who heard her ex-husband say she was a bad parent even though I had heard something completely different. I guarantee that this exact same thing will happen with you as well. But, your brain will tell you in each instance that you are seeing Reality. *Not true*!

You need to be flexible enough with your ideas so that they can allow for positive change. You need to remain aware that, as a human being with a big, and wonderfully complex brain, you will have predictable shifts in perspective that, under stress, shift in a negative direction. You are wired to see your ex as more evil, stupid, and crazy than he or she really is and to see them that way even after they have cleaned up their act. You have to be willing to imagine that sometimes you are not seeing totally objectively. And, you must persevere. This is because even if you are pointed in the right direction and taking the right steps, it will seem like you aren't. The next section of this chapter will help you recognize negative thought patterns to help you steer toward objectivity and positivity.

So, the point of this discussion is that we are wired to have certain perceptual shifts when under stress. They are not random, but predictable. This predictability can work to our advantage. Imagine two cars. One pulls strongly to the left while you drive it. The other pulls randomly both left and right and to various degrees. If you had to rush you're your child to the emergency room with a broken arm, which car would you drive?

As humans, we inherit a complex physical stress reaction. This fight-or-flight response served our ancestors well, but mostly gets in the way because we mostly deal with non-physical threats. As separated parents, we must keep our mental and emotional strengths online to establish an effective co-parenting relationship. High stress inhibits the parts of our brain devoted to thinking and feelings processes that we need to do our best job. I have described some of the common mental effects that result from these brain changes. Let's review them…

> - Your brain is wired to seek a sense of control and, when you feel out of control, you get more stressed
> - If you don't have an objective explanation of your experience, your brain makes up and explanation
> - Your brain focuses on data that supports the explanation
> - The part of your brain that thinks positively, creatively, and about the future shuts down under stress
> - You are wired to react quickly to danger; but the slower parts of your brain are needed for optimal co-parenting
> - You are wired to think things are more important and urgent than they objectively are
> - You are wired to stay fixated on negative thoughts and emotions triggered by separation-related adjustments
> - Any random input can trigger: This is Hell, because my ex is Evil, Stupid, and Crazy, and let me tell you about it!
> - Expect artifacts from the past
> - During stressful conflicts, you may lose sight of innocent bystanders—your children

The bad news is that your brain, like mine, and everyone else's, is wired this way. The good news is that knowing about it can help us correct for these effects. Because these effects produce predictable issues for separating parents, there are strategies you can employ that take care of them. Partly, it is just being aware that the effects exist. But, there are some specific things you can do to dial down the negative consequences of the stress reaction. I don't want you to get in the car that pulls to the left and just drive off the road to the left. I want you to use the strategies I'll explain throughout the rest of the book to stay on track.

# 3 ANTIDOTES TO TROUBLED THINKING

In the previous chapter, I explained several effects that stress has on your brain. You may have already been aware of some of them, or at least noticed how they manifest in your—and your ex's—behaviors. These effects are the explanation for why seemingly functional people get involved in unending post-separation conflicts. They spiral into unsatisfying fights over pretty much anything and everything. Their other relationships with co-workers, neighbors, new partners, extended family, and even random strangers on the street look relatively positive and normal. But, put the two of them in the same place at the same time and you see all hell break loose! Don't let this be you!

I believe in your capacity to be positive and creative and to focus appropriately on a desirable future for you and your children. But, sometimes your strengths are getting derailed temporarily. Unfortunately, they are often derailed when you really need them. So, here are my recommendations to dial down these effects. You should understand that these only work when you *actually practice them*. Some parts of this material can be helpful if they make you more insightful into your situation. But, if you do everything next week exactly the same way you did this week, well…next week is going to look pretty much like this week. Put these into practice to get the benefits.

*Levels of Response*

Michael Olpin and Margie Hesson, in their book *Stress Management for Life*, offer an excellent explanation of how thought patterns and stress interact. Stress results in negative thinking. Negative thinking results in higher stress. It's a reflexive cycle that can spiral toward unsatisfying outcomes. Learning to recognize these response levels is a key to keeping more of the positive part of your brain online. And, understanding the various levels of response is a practical strategy to see that there is more than one way to perceive and react to "reality." Some types of response lead to effective coping and others don't.

The levels of response can be divided into three categories: negative, neutral, and positive. Negative thoughts lead away from optimal coping. They increase stress and make satisfying solutions less likely. They lead to conflict, mistrust, anger, and frustration. Neutral thoughts help unhook you from stress and negative thoughts and make positive responses possible. Neutral responses lead to calmness and inquiry into possibilities. Positive thoughts counteract stress and negative thinking. They actually lead to joy and hope. Olpin and Hesson divide these three types of thinking further.

> **Negative Responses**
> Attachment/Correctness
> Judgment/Criticism/Blaming
> Complaining
>
> **Neutral Responses**
> Observation
> Discovery
>
> **Positive Responses**
> Acceptance
> Gratitude

Let me explain how these different response levels are all available in the same situation. I'll use a situation that happened to me recently. I was walking across the university campus with my Labrador Retriever, Annie, who sometimes goes to class with me. She had stopped to poop when we had first gotten close to campus. However, as we neared the building in which I was about to teach, she stopped at a small grassy area near a busy sidewalk—hundreds of students were rushing by—to poop, again. One objective situation (to a neutral observer, maybe), but several potential "realities" for me, depending on my type of response. Here are the thoughts at each level that could have run through my head.

**Attachment/Correctness:** *No! Don't poop, again! I have to be in class in five minutes! You already pooped just a few minutes ago! You can't have more poop in there! And, not here in front of hundreds of students! They might be thinking I'm not going to clean it up and are thinking I'm a disgusting person for bringing my dog on campus. I don't want to have to set my coffee and book bag down to clean this up. I want to be walking into class right now!*

**Judgment/Criticism/Blaming:** *Bad dog! You shouldn't be pooping, again! You should have waited until after class! You're going to make me late! You're embarrassing me! You should have gotten all that poop out when you pooped 20 minutes ago! You could have knocked the coffee out of my hand when you suddenly veered off our walking path into the grass!*

**Complaining:** *This sucks! I want to be walking into class right now, not standing here with Annie pooping in front of all these students. I don't want to have to clean up a second poop. Being a dog-owner sucks right now.*

**Observation:** *She's pooping twice in 20 minutes. She usually poops about once or twice per day. It doesn't appear that she's sick since both poops looked pretty normal. People don't seem to be taking much notice of Annie and, certainly, aren't frowning at me. I notice Annie always has that dopey look on her face while she's pooping.*

**Creativity:** *It's interesting that she's pooping, again. She just pooped a really big poop just minutes ago. I wonder how many times she can poop in a single day? She pees on command. I wonder if it's possible to teach a dog to poop on command?*

**Acceptance:** *Part of taking a dog to class includes giving her opportunities to poop when she needs to. This is normal dog behavior. It's taking only a couple of minutes and I have five more in which to get to the classroom. I can wait while she poops. And, I have a plastic bag to clean up her poop.*

**Gratitude:** *Boy, I'm glad you pooped out here, before class, and not in the classroom! It's good that you are pooping on grass, rather than the sidewalk. And, I'm really happy I have a plastic bag with me so people don't step in it! And, it's great that there's a trash can about thirty feet away, so I don't have to carry this bag of poop around with me. I'm also glad that when she veered off our path, she didn't pull the leash and knock the coffee out of my hand (something which has happened before).*

One objective reality can lead to a wide range of responses which lead to different stress levels and behavioral reactions. And, it doesn't just impact the immediate situation. My frame of mind when I walk into class is dependent on how I respond to the pooping situation. Thinking about that situation, now, outside of the moment, I see that being negative wouldn't have been useful. There really wasn't anything Annie should have been doing differently. And, it wasn't really a crisis. I had plenty of time to get to class, the poop got cleaned up, and nobody even seemed to be taking much notice of us. (I'll tell you that my thought process in the actual moment went like this: I immediately noticed attachment/judgment/critical thinking pop into my head. Then, I followed that with the thoughts related to observation, creativity, acceptance, and gratitude. It wasn't that the negative thoughts weren't there, but that I saw them as thoughts, not reality. When you're not caught in "reality", you can keep on thinking and move to more positive, creative, helpful thoughts. I was actually smiling at the end of it, especially after thinking how much better it was for Annie to be pooping *before* and not *during* class!)

These levels of response are relevant to situations when dealing with separation and interacting with your other parent. It is easy for your stressed-out brain to focus on the three negative levels of response. As I have explained before, the parts of your brain devoted to the neutral and positive responses actually get inhibited during higher stress. So, that type of more helpful thinking doesn't come naturally. You have to train yourself to notice the negative, unhelpful response. Know that that is only one version of reality and the range of possible responses. And, then choose to shift your thinking so you are less stressed and actually responding with effective coping. The neutral and positive response levels will lead to better coping (calm down, clean up the poop, proceed to class on time). The negative ones aren't just subjectively less fun. They don't instrumentally help the situation. Too often parents are stuck in these three negative levels, saying to each other various versions of: *This shouldn't be happening this way! You suck! And, this whole situation sucks!*

The negative types of thinking aren't just unhelpful. They lead in a downward spiral. If you only think in those negative modes, you will get locked into lasting conflicts, unable to shift your co-parenting relationship in a more positive direction. Both of them are having negative responses which aren't instrumentally helpful and which feed into their shared negativity. However important the issue at hand and however legitimate a criticism is of the other parent, you and your children will not be well served if you two primarily respond with the three negative levels. But, it doesn't have to be that way.

Learn to see those initial, negative, gut-reactions as options, not the only reality. This will be challenging until you practice it for some time. So many times parents want to come to my office and primarily complain about each other to me. They are very aware of their attachments: *This should be this way! That should be that way!* And, they fight with each other, telling each other all the ways they suck as co-parents. And, they tell themselves that they won't be able to make it better. A hopeless situation!

I think this is normal. But, it is something to change. Probably, over time, when things are more stable and your stress level starts to subside, you and the other parent will naturally drift toward more positive thinking and responses. This is a common trend with most (about two-thirds) separated parents (though many parents don't do this...about one-third). However, this shift doesn't happen soon enough. You need relief from the stress of negative responses. And, your children need you two to be effective co-parents now. So, don't delay. Practice shifting toward the positive end. Here's an exercise to help you do that.

> ### Levels of Response Exercise
>
> **1:** Think of a recent situation you found challenging. It doesn't have to be a situation with the other parent. Choose something that is somewhat resolved and not currently highly triggering.
>
> **2:** Get out a notebook. Write a response to the situation from each of the levels. Do as I did when describing the situation with my dog. It may be initially challenging to think from some of those angles. But, it is good to practice being flexible with your thinking. Every time you do this, you strengthen the part of your brain which thinks more creatively and positively. You also come to know that these different response levels are each a choice among several very different responses. It will lead to increasingly effective responses in real situations.
>
> **3:** Repeat! This technique may be helpful to know about. But, the goal is only partly to have the insight that one can have different responses. The goal is to actually employ this shift in thinking in real situations. And, you will only get better if you actually practice it. This will be challenging to do if you wait to try to use it first in a highly triggering interaction with your other parent. Practice it in other realms of your life until it becomes easier to do. Practice. Practice. Practice!

*Get Good Sleep*

Don't underestimate the importance of getting good sleep. You might dismiss this advice because you think that either it's just general well-wishing or things are so out of your control that you can't do anything to increase your ongoing sleep quality. Certainly, your life is likely complicated and full, right now. You might prefer to get more sleep because you'll feel better. But, you may not know just how important it is and that good sleep relates to all of the stress effects discussed in this book.

Getting good sleep does make you feel good, physically. Most of our detoxification and repair at the cellular level takes place during sleep. When we are awake, even if not very active, we build up toxins in our body. These toxins result in that tired feeling. The detoxing and repair that occurs during sleep is why we wake up feeling refreshed, physically. Being chronically sleep-deprived puts one at risk of diseases that are caused by these toxins. None of us want to feel chronically tired, but there are other reasons sleep is important for separated parents.

Sleep deprivation is shown to have many negative effects on brain states including, reducing auditory attention, making it harder to complete tasks that require divided attention, making it more likely that distractions will draw our attention away from what we're trying to focus on, making us less capable of appropriately shifting between multiple tasks as the situation might need, making us perform worse at tasks that require us to combine a lot of complex elements in order to make an important decision, making us less creative and innovative, increasing our engaging in risky behavior, making us poorer at tasks that involve thinking ahead and planning, making us less likely to learn from mistakes and correct our behavior in a repeated situation, reducing our ability to transfer our experience into meaningful memories that serve us in the future, and increasing our stress response. Sleep is not completely understood, though research has shown that poor sleep is associated with many of the same negative health effects of chronic stress. Sleep deprived individuals are more likely to have the fight-or-flight response. Sleep deprivation triggers the immune system in the same way that the stress response does. Part of what is known is that these effects are mediated by changing activity in the prefrontal cortex—*the same part of the brain that you need for perceiving and responding well to the complexities of separated parenting!* There is a biological reason for the phrase, *Let's sleep on it*. Your ability to think and feel positively is mediated by certain neurotransmitters (including dopamine and serotonin) that get regenerated mostly while you are asleep.

So, with each of the negative effects that result from high stress, you could substitute *sleep-deprivation*. It has the same effects. And, it helps trigger your stress response, which increases the negative brain effects. All while putting your health at risk. Not a good situation.

Bad sleep comes in many forms. Some people have trouble falling asleep. Others wake in the middle of the night, or early in the morning, and have trouble getting back to sleep. Sometimes people sleep a normal sleep cycle, but don't wake feeling rested. There is no one type of sleep dysfunction and no simple general fix. But, here are some tips.

Identify ways that your choices support, or undermine, good sleep. If you get regularly involved in channel surfing when you could go to bed, shift that pattern and choose to sleep, instead. If there are environmental factors that interrupt your sleep, and which you can control, change them. If, for example, your cat is waking you up in the middle of the night, lock it in the basement or somewhere out of earshot. Some people benefit from playing low-level music to provide white noise which lessens the interrupting effects of extraneous sounds. Taking a ten to twenty minute nap during the day can be a way to make up for lost sleep. Do something relaxing, rather than energizing, before going to bed. Practicing the stress management techniques described in this book or doing fifteen minutes of yoga would be better than playing video games or watching a thriller on television. Take a hot bath. Masturbate.

If you are losing sleep because you are fretting about life complications, I offer these strategies: Before you go to bed, acknowledge that you have some worries and that you can deal with them the next day. Scheduling a time to come back around to an issue sometimes allows our brain to unhook. Keep a notebook by your bed. If you wake during the night and think of something that might be important, write it down. That way, you can come back to it later and don't have to stay more wakeful to keep it in the front of your mind. It works the same as writing groceries on your shopping list so you don't have to spend mental energy trying to not forget all the items. You write them down, then let go of them.

To some degree, we can bank sleep to the next night by getting extra hours. However, extra sleep doesn't carry very far into the future. And, we can make up for lost sleep pretty readily if we have a bad night. But, chronic bad sleep will add up in terms of stress and more emotional swings. Some people experiment with drugs to aid sleep quality. There are prescribed and over-the-counter drugs that have a sedative effect some people find helpful. I caution you in the use of drugs for sleep. One of the most common strategies I see in stressed out separated parents is drinking alcohol. While alcohol does sedate people and make it easier to fall asleep, it tends to interfere with sleep quality. Many people don't end up feeling rested the next morning if falling asleep aided by alcohol. In general, I discourage drinking to deal with post-separation stress. Some of the other drugs leave people feeling a bit hung over in the morning, too, especially those with longer actions. You may want to discuss the issue with your doctor if you are experiencing chronic sleep disturbance, though if you do, I strongly encourage you to seek good medical management of those drugs as some are addictive or have problematic side effects.

Become better aware of the connection between your sleep quality and your mental and emotional functioning. Having a better awareness of this connection can help you when you need to choose when and how to respond to a co-parenting complication. In general,

I recommend avoiding challenging interactions later in the day. Being tired is about the same as being sleep deprived. Even if you are generally sleeping OK, if you are like most people, you don't perform as well when you are tired. Schedule communications and interactions with your other parent earlier in the day. Also, for non-urgent issues that can be delayed, if it's a day after a bad night of sleep, consider putting them off until you are more rested.

*Reduce Your Caffeine Intake*

Caffeine can be a problem when you are attempting to lower your stress. A member of a class of so-called *sympathomimetic* chemicals, it directly stimulates the physical components of the fight-or-flight response. It can do this, even in moments when you aren't particularly stressed. A recent study showed that amounts of caffeine equivalent of five to eight cups of coffee can induce panic attacks in people who aren't otherwise in a stressful situation.

If you are a regular drinker of caffeinated beverages, you may think that your moderate intake doesn't result in your feeling stressed out. However, even if you are somewhat tolerant because of regular intake, any dose of caffeine contributes to the potential of a stress response. More caffeine equals more potential. Since your current level of stress should probably be lower (to avoid those unhelpful stress-related brain effects or other reasons), you should consider experimenting with cutting down on your daily caffeine intake.

Do not quick caffeine cold turkey if you have been using it for a long period of time at a moderate to high level. Sudden caffeine withdrawal results in a flu-like syndrome that, while not life-threatening, is unpleasant. These symptoms don't tend to happen if you taper off, slowly. Caffeine potentiates stress. It also, for many people, interferes with sleep quality.

# 4 TOP SIX STRATEGIES

In this chapter I'll describe six powerful strategies to help you co-parent more effectively. They include: clarification, time-out, thankfulness, empathy, a focus on the present, and paying attention to the Big Trigger. Like the strategies discussed in the previous chapter, they serve as the antidotes to common pitfalls for separated parents.

*Top Strategy One: Clarification*

Have you ever played the game *telephone*? If so, you know that even among friends, and with content that is not loaded with strong emotion, communication can easily become derailed. That's the purpose of the game and the source of the fun. But, as we have discussed, your brain is wired to not have accurate perceptions when under high stress. And, pretty much all of the content separated parent choose to discuss is very loaded. Miscommunications and misunderstandings will happen often, even more often than in the low-stress situation of a game of *telephone* at summer camp. Miscommunication is to be expected. It is not failure, unless you don't attempt to correct it.

Back to the game of *telephone*. You are allowed, in some versions of the game to call *operator*. This means that the person who just whispered the sentence in your ear will repeat it one more time. You call "operator" and they whisper for the second time, *The fuzzy cat ran under the porch* (or whatever the sentence might be at that point in the game). But, in the game telephone, you are not allowed to turn to the person before you and clarify by asking, *I think you said, "The fuzzy cat ran under the porch." Is that right?*

Practicing clarification will ruin the fun of the game *telephone* because it would mean that the sentence couldn't possibly get messed up. The fun is that the sentence becomes nonsense by the end of the line. But the thing that will ruin the fun and games at summer camp is the very thing you need to be doing with your other parent.

Imagine two parents who have had a discussion about switching the parenting time schedule. At the end of the conversation, for whatever reason, both parents are thinking that at the end of their daughter's basketball game at her school, she will go home with them. There has been a misunderstanding. But this doesn't become apparent until after the game when the parents get into a fight in front of the daughter and several of her friends in the parking lot. This could have been avoided.

At the end of the initial conversation between the parents, one of them could have said, *So, as I understand it, she will go home with me directly after the game. Is that right?* If the other parent wasn't thinking that, then they could have continued to discuss it. Another way to reinforce this strategy is a feature of the business model of co-parenting popularized by Isolina Ricci's book *Mom's House Dad's House*. That is to say at the end of the conversation, *OK. So, we have an agreement. I'll text/e-mail you tonight just to confirm it.*

Clarification often feels awkward at first. This is because we don't tend to communicate this way and usually just put up with some amount of miscommunications. But, in a co-parenting relationship that is so full of negotiations around so many things and between two people whose brains are working against them, it is essential. If you tell me that you encounter miscommunications ten percent (or less) of the time and, when it happens, you never end up in a fight in front of (or within earshot) of your children, then go ahead and skip this strategy. But, if you are encountering not being on the same page often and sometimes get into conflicts around your children because of it, do it. Clarify often until it no longer feels weird.

*Top Strategy Two: Time-out*

When we get triggered, we tend to have a quick spike in stress which subsides to a lower level, eventually coming back down to our pre-spike baseline. Of course, this cycle depends on the situation and our general pattern of reacting to stress. But, it is useful to know what our individual cycle looks like. Some people calm down a notch or two in a few seconds. Others take minutes, or hours. In an ideal world, we learn to do this calming down more quickly. But, we all go through this type of reactive cycle.

You can work with this predictable reaction cycle by choosing, at least sometimes, to avoid reacting during that early peak of stress and emotion. In terms of behaving in a clear and civil manner, our brains are in their least helpful mode when our stress is at the highest level. If the building is on fire, we just have to go with it and react anyway. But, 99% of the time the building is not on fire and waiting some time before reacting will be of great benefit. More of your frontal lobe will come online and you'll have a more optimal reaction.

Time-out should not only be a tool in your tool box but, you should practice it regularly. In fact, until you practice it several times, it will feel awkward and won't seem to work in the way you want it to. It's kind of like learning to ride a bicycle. An explanation of the method doesn't really help and you can't do it well until you try it several times and actually get it to work the way you want. After that, it works very well. The good news is: it's hard to unlearn how to ride a bicycle once you've learned it. The same holds for time-out. Here are my suggestions about how to make this strategy most effective.

First, if possible, discuss this as a conscious, intentional strategy that you and the other parent will employ from time to time. You need to both know that it is a specific strategy that one of you will suggest in moments when one or both of you are triggered and you think that you will be better served by stopping the interaction temporarily. If your other parent doesn't seem willing to be on board with this strategy, it is still useful and I suggest that you explain to him/her that you intend to sometimes call for a time-out in order to not react too negatively.

One caveat with the use of this strategy is that you should ideally use it as a *delay* of an interaction, not merely to *stop* a reaction. If calling a time-out is really code for, *Shut up, I'm not going to deal with this!*, then your ex will not soon respect your call for a time-out. You must be forthright and call a time-out with the intention of coming back around to the discussion later, but soon. Know the difference between calling a time-out and communicating that you will not address a particular issue at all. I know this particular advice will be challenging for you if your primary conflict-resolution strategy is avoidance. If that describes you, then you probably already put off dealing with conflicts, so your ex is not going to be quickly trusting given your likely history. But, it is still a good idea and I strongly suggest you start employing it.

Another challenge with starting to experiment with this strategy is that the first several times one of you calls time-out, it won't seem to work. You and the other parent have a significant history of unresolved conflicts. The first few times you, or they, call for a time-out, the other one will hear it as, *Shut up, I'm not going to deal with this!* They will hear it as a *shutting down*, not *delaying* of the conversation. They will only begin to hear it as a legitimate call for a time-out if you actually come back to the issue when you've calmed down. And, they probably won't begin to hear it that way until you've done it several times. So, if you try to employ time-out and it doesn't seem to be working, keep doing it. Even if you do it correctly, it is not likely to work the first few times you employ it. And, even if your other parent doesn't really like your calling for a time-out, it may lead to better outcomes if you, or they, actually calm down a bit before you proceed with the conversation.

Practice, practice, practice! Remember how many times you climbed onto your first bicycle before you were comfortable riding. And, now think about how enjoyable it is to ride around. Get through the first part of practicing this strategy and you'll greatly benefit later.

When I am working with parents directly, I ask them to intentionally practice time-out several times over one or two weeks, even in low-level situations when they don't think they need to. Think of it this way: If you pull the strategy out for the first time when it is crucial, you are employing it for initial practice in a very difficult moment for you and the other parent. It is likely to fail. But, if you use time-out for some relatively trivial, non-urgent issues for practice, it will be easier to employ in more critical moments. In a less-triggering, non-urgent situation it is much easier to hear from the other parent, *Hey, why don't we talk about this, again, later this evening when we're both more calm?* It's just the same as learning bicycle riding on easy terrain rather than a steep, dangerous mountain-bike trail.

*Top Strategy Three: Thankfulness*

You may not immediately like this suggestion, but I'm going to encourage you to do it anyway. First, it might sound as though I'm treating you like a toddler (because that's the age at which we start asking children to say *please* and *thank you*). Or, you might think I'm asking you to paint a rosy picture and ignore all the crap you get from the other parent. I don't mean to treat you like a child and, I don't want to trivialize the issues in your life. And, this is an extremely powerful strategy. I strongly encourage you to practice it often.

If you remember my discussion of the pie chart, I said that one problem with ongoing conflicts between parents is that they view the other parent mostly, or totally, as a source of divorce hell. There is no green slice. This is largely an effect of perception. But, you can influence the actual data the other parent has to work with by offering something for their green slice.

Now, I'll acknowledge that one reason you might not thank each other is that when the other parent does something you like, you might think, *Well, that's what they should have done, and they should have been doing that all along.* As an example, I worked with a set of parents and an ongoing issue was that one parent usually didn't have the children ready for pick-up until ten to twenty minutes after the agree-upon time. The other parent would arrive on time and had to sit, waiting, in the driveway for the kids to be ready.

When the parent who often didn't have the children ready *did* get them out of the door relatively on time, the parent who was waiting wasn't in a thankful mood. He was thinking, *Well, good that this is happening, but it should be happening all the time like this.* He only said something when he complained about the lack of punctuality. Now you might argue that the one parent should have had the children ready most of the time anyway and, I would agree with you. But, only complaining when there is a failure to meet expectations serves to only deliver negativity. If the on-time parent was pointing out the lateness *and* the times when it worked as scheduled, that would be a different mix of positive and negative feedback. That is much more helpful.

Thanking is clearer feedback than complaining. It's a better way to let someone know about something that is important to you. I'll give you a recent example from my life. Our daughter was with me one afternoon. The plan was to take her to her mother's office at 5:00 p.m. when she finished work. At 4:30, I got a call from her mother saying she was in a meeting that would go late and asking if I could come and hour later at 6:00. I said I could and did. Two days later, I got an e-mail from my ex-wife thanking me for making that last minute schedule change. It felt nice to get that e-mail. And, it gave me some clear feedback about something that she thought was important—having a flexible, reciprocal relationship that can accommodate changes.

Remember the last time someone thanked you for something. It felt good. It burns nearly zero calories to deliver a thank you. And yet, it is so very beneficial to good relationships. When the other parent does something that you value, thank them. They may not know what to make of it the first two or three times you do this, but that's OK. Just keep doing it. You're unlikely to piss them off by doing it, and it may be of great benefit. I think so.

*Top Strategy Four: Empathy*

Empathy is the sense of emotional and psychological connection to another person. It is often used synonymously with sympathy which is the sharing of concern for someone. We naturally have empathy for people with whom we share a positive relationship or a relationship in which we strongly want to pursue shared goals (for example, salespeople often exhibit empathy with potential clients). Empathy functions as the glue that helps tie people together in friend, community, and family relationships. It can be a powerful motivator for us to act in support of another person's interests, even if different from ours (we take time from a busy day to talk to a friend who is feeling sad). It fuels positive regard for others. And, in relationships that are net-negative and fraught with unresolved conflict, it goes completely out the window.

You aren't dysfunctional if you don't feel empathy toward your other parent. However, having empathy toward your child's other parent is instrumentally very helpful for at least two reasons. Generating and expressing empathy can clue you in to important information about her or him. And, expressing empathy is another powerful technique to create the green slice and to help your other parent have a sense that their interests are being heard.

When we feel empathy toward another person, we generate a rich, internal understanding of their experience. Now, that internal representation is probably, at best, an approximation. But, it foster's a sense of shared connection. It also causes us to "know" something about what the other person is thinking and feeling. When we feel sad when talking to our sad friend, it's not precisely the same sadness, but close enough. We share the feeling quality and those congruent feelings help us make sense of their words and actions. Brain research has identified parts of the brain devoted to empathy and special pathways of mirror neurons which cause us to have that shared sense of reality.

Empathy is about the present moment. Regardless of past experiences, empathy is about what a person is *currently* thinking and feeling. Empathy can be a tool for getting out of the past and responding more effectively in the present moment. I'm guessing that you would tell me that you know a lot about your other parent. You have a rich, shared history. You have, more recently, come to know each other as separated parents. So, even if the other parent were absent, you could tell me a lot about him or her. This information would be partially relevant. But, unless you are psychic, you couldn't tell me what their actual current thoughts and emotions were. This is the importance of empathy. Your current, real-time, thoughts and emotions matter. And, so do those of your other parent. To ignore what your other parent is thinking or feeling is to set yourself up for unending conflict. You will doom yourself to only having a relationship with the person of the past. You will ignore information that you need in order to make good choices on your end of things (such as, I see that the other parent seems to be having a really bad day so this probably isn't the best moment to raise a complex, and potentially triggering, issue). You will tend to have a stereotypical response pattern, rather than one that is more dependent on current circumstances. And, ignoring this useful information, will more likely have the experience of being blind-sided by surprising behaviors.

The other important aspect of empathy toward the other parent is that it makes it more likely they will have a sense that you understand them, that you are paying attention, that they have been heard during consequential interactions. Everybody wants to have a sense of being heard. Even when others don't agree with us, it is somewhat satisfying if they demonstrate that they are listening meaningfully to us. I see this commonly during mediation sessions. Parents who actually hear and reflect each other's concerns have a much lower level of conflict than those who don't. An example of this was during a recent mediation session when during a conflict over post-divorce financial asset sharing, the ex-husband said to the ex-wife, *Look, I know that you are worried that you aren't going to have enough monthly income to stay in the house where you're currently living.* It wasn't that he was interested in making it possible for her to stay in that house. In fact, he was proposing to sell the house to split the equity. But, he acknowledged her thoughts and feelings in regards to the matter. Even though they were in conflict over positions (sell the house or not), she knew that he understood her concerns and motivation to try to keep the house. This seemed less triggering for her than it would have been if he had just discounted, or ignored, her experience. Don't underestimate the value of empathy in your interactions.

I'm not suggesting you have empathy by actually becoming friends. As I have said before, being friends may not be the best goal, at least in the short-term. And, even if that eventually unfolds for you, you need to be functional co-parents right now. You can't wait. And, I'm not suggesting that you act like you have positive regard for or agreement with the other parent when you actually don't. They probably know you well enough to see through that, anyway.

What I invite you to do is this. Notice that you (like all of us humans), don't feel empathy when you're triggered and dealing with the person who is triggering you. Remember that, perhaps, in many situations, it's fine if empathy goes out the window. But, in this situation, you're dealing with someone around the welfare of your child. This is so important, you need to bring empathy back online in order to make good choices on your end of the dynamic and to steer toward a more functional co-parenting relationship. Then, consider the words your other parent is saying. However difficult it is for you to listen to them, those words give you clues about what is important to them. Notice their non-verbal behavior. This information helps you know something about which emotions they are currently feeling and how strong they are. Take ten to fifteen minutes sometimes when you are not interacting with them (or anyone else) and contemplate what your co-parenting situation would be like from their perspective. All of this will take effort. You might not even be able to do it at first. However, you have the capacity to do this, at least some of the time. You don't even have to think of it as something you do to benefit the other parent. It is for your, and your child's, benefit to pay careful attention to all relevant information that can help you make the wisest choices on your end of the co-parenting dynamic.

Dealing with your other parent's emotions can be tricky. Certainly, as separated parents, you are renegotiating emotional boundaries. It isn't your job, now, to take care of your other parent's emotions in the same way you might have done when you were intimate partners. And, it isn't wise to ignore their emotions, altogether. You will have to find the middle ground. The next chapter will explore issues related to emotions further.

*Top Strategy Five: Focus on the Present, Not the Past*

Parents sometimes think past issues must be resolved in order to deal effectively with each other as separated co-parents. The short answer: No, you don't. But, let me explain in more detail.

The concern about having to resolve the past comes from two incorrect assumptions. One is based on psychodynamic theories (mostly based on Freud's writings) which emphasize stages of development. Stage models say that you can't navigate a later stage if you didn't successfully complete the former ones. This idea is not well-supported by research or lived experience. Some things do build on previous experiences. But, not all of life is perfectly sequenced. We often muddle through, even when we don't do a perfect job. We sometimes go back and clean up past messes.

The psychodynamic model goes like this: You have inner psychological dynamics that result in your having certain experiences and behavioral patterns. If you want those to change, you must explore those inner experiences to re-work them. Perhaps this model has served some people well. But, know that it is a long process. Traditional psychoanalysis was expected to take twenty to thirty years to cure a neurosis. You don't have that much time. Your children certainly can't wait that long for you to get your act together.

Cognitive-Behavioral approaches offer another perspective. Cognitive theories say that you can shift your cognitions in a short period of time, regardless of the inner dynamics which influence them. For example, I want you to shift your attention to the movement of your belly as you take your next couple of breaths. Notice the expansion and contraction below your diaphragm. You made that shift in less than a second. You didn't have to lie on a couch for numerous sessions exploring why you are, or aren't, the type of person who notices the body movements associated with your breathing. I asked you to shift, and you did. Many cognitive processes are like this and these ideas provide the basis for my approach described in this book.

Behavioral approaches also offer relatively rapid change. You might have heard this joke: *Patient: Doctor, my arm hurts when I move it like this. Doctor: Don't move it like that!* This is the behavioral approach. The doctor didn't say, lie down on that couch and we'll talk for twenty years about why you have that pain in your arm when you move it like that. Sometimes insight into the past simply won't help. If you have a flat tire, all the insight in the world about how you came to run over that nail won't help you. Getting out and changing the tire will help you move on down the road. The point is: You choose a new behavioral pattern that works for you. Either you can see what that new pattern is, or not. Either you can do it, or you can't. Discern it, then put it into practice. Don't wait until you know all the reasons for it. There is an old story in Buddhist teachings about this.

> *A man is shot by a poisoned arrow on the battlefield. When his colleagues rush to pull out the arrow, he refuses, wanting them to wait to pull it out until he knows who shot it, and why, and so on. He dies before he gets his questions answered.*

Often it is better to just pull out the arrow. Worry about the explanation later (or not at all).

Because you were in an intimate relationship with your other parent, you have focused quite strongly, perhaps for a very long period of time, on trying to understand why you each have experienced what you have and behaved the way that you did. This is normal. In the context of that former relationship, that type of thinking made sense. It might have contributed to different outcomes. But, you are no longer engaged in the goals of long-term, shared intimacy. You might continue to ponder these issues. In the future, this contemplation might result in some useful insights. Perhaps it will help you in a future relationship. Having that type of strong focus has momentum and you will probably have the urge to continue. But, you do not need to solve those issues to move forward as functional co-parents.

The other incorrect assumption is that separated co-parenting is the same as an intimate partnership. It isn't. It's a different ball game. I often hear parents say, *Well, if we would have had the skills to be good co-parents, we wouldn't have gotten divorced!* The implication is that their failed relationship is proof that they will fail as separated parents. They sometimes mean that their relationship post-separation is marked with hostility and poor communication and cooperation. If they would have been more friendly, communicative, and cooperative, they would still be married. Well, maybe, and maybe not. I think sometimes the focus on dysfunction patterns during, or after, the break-up ignores other, fundamental problems with the relationship (for example, diverging relationship goals). If two parents are so lacking in relationship skills, how do we explain the early months/years, before it all went south?

I do think that some issues that might have gotten in the way of satisfying and lasting shared intimacy can pose challenges for co-parenting. Substance abuse, mental health issues, interpersonal violence, economic stress, and other stressors create challenges before, and after, separation. However, new boundaries and lack of intimate involvement may provide a buffer for some of these issues.

Certainly some elements of a rewarding intimate partnership overlap with a functional co-parenting relationship. Positive regard, respect, trust, clear and civil communication, support. You might name others. These are core building blocks for many types of relationships, not just intimate and co-parenting relationships. I would say that these things are very desirable in a relationship with a co-worker or even a housemate. I want my co-workers to view me positively, be respectful, trustworthy, and supportive. I want them to be clear and civil communicators. But, I wouldn't necessarily want to marry all of my co-workers! It's not the same. The fact that these elements are essential to a variety of relationships doesn't make them all the same. Different types of relationships with unique sets of shared goals determine what will be needed to sustain them. Your former partnership with your child's other parent provided its unique rewards and challenges. It was not sustained, but that doesn't doom the two of you to failure at co-parenting. Even if, looking back, you diagnose your relationship as being particularly lacking in these essential elements, you two can develop these now that you are separated. Some parents find it an easier task to do that *after* separation. In any case, I discourage you from trying to resolve past issues in order to focus on the present tasks of shared co-parenting. If you make resolving the past a prerequisite, you will unnecessarily delay a proper focus on co-parenting.

A pitfall related to focusing on the past is trying to sort out blame. People get mired in a conflict over "reality." That is, two people argue over who was right, or who is correct in their description of the history of the relationship. This is a bottomless pit. Please try to not fall into it. It often sounds like this: *We're divorced because you cheated on me. Well, I had that affair because we never had sex. Well, I never felt like having sex with someone who was a jerk all the time. Well, I would have been nicer to you, if you would've been home more rather than always at work. Well, I worked those extra hours because of all the money you spent.* That type of argument has no end, even if you think you're right.

Years after separation, many separated couples are probably still working with radically different stories about the relationship and why it ended. I believe that is OK. It may be desirable on some level to negotiate agreement about what happened. When people are in more agreement about shared history, we do see less conflict. But, it isn't essential. It most cases, it simply isn't going to happen. And, your children don't need you to have this type of agreement in order to functionally co-parent them. Drop it. Your children have needs now, and into the future. The past is finished. You don't have access to it, anyway. If you are focused on the past, you will not be here in the present. And, this type of focus on the past only leads to more, not less, conflict. It will get in the way of focusing on the present.

When you were still partners, I believe each of you had a responsibility to each other to work out a mutually acceptable reality. Not in a pure sense, as I believe that's not attainable. But, I do think it's reasonable to want, generally, to be on the same page with your partner. There are many different versions of *intimacy* but, I think most would have that element. However, now that you are separated, the boundaries are different. As separated parents, it isn't essential for you two to work out this type of close, shared reality about the past. It's valuable for a sense of intimacy in a romantic relationship, but only will get in the way in your current situation. Your ex does not have a responsibility to you to work out a shared understanding of your former relationship. Because you share a child (or children), you each have a lot of co-parenting responsibilities. But, those unrelated to co-parenting–mostly about your former relationship—are over. Let go of them and focus on the present. Save that type of contemplation and processing for sessions with your individual therapist. Don't bring them up to your ex.

Most, if not all, separated parents are thinking about past issues in their heads. This is normal. But, to maintain a more functional co-parenting dynamic, avoid focusing on the past. The past is often the content of complaints, which I think are unhelpful. I'll discuss avoiding complaining in the next two chapters.

*Top Strategy Six: Pay Attention to The BIG TRIGGER!*

There are many things your ex and you find triggering about each other. There will be many things each of you perceive in the other in your attempts to co-parent which will be triggering. Your ex will do things you'll find challenging. You will do things your ex will find challenging. But, few triggers, if any, will push your buttons more than perceiving the other parent as keeping you from your child. I call this *The Big Trigger.*

I assume there is nothing in your life you hold more dear than your child. You value your relationship with your child. You are highly committed to your parenting role. You would do almost anything to keep your child safe and thriving. Each of us is wired to behave this way. Evolution endowed us with serious brain circuits devoted to attachment to the parenting role. This is a good thing as it keeps us in the game even when parenting is wildly challenging. Without this wiring, our ancestors might have given up on the task.

In the context of separated parenting, this wiring might be helpful in motivating us to face the challenges and complexity of dealing with separation and crafting a co-parenting relationship. And, it provides a mechanism for conflict. This is because the separation of your homes necessarily results in barriers between each of you and your child. If you or your ex see the fact of the separation as the other parent's fault, then this is viewed as a threat to contact with the child. Failure to optimally co-parent after separation further exacerbates this issue. The higher your conflict and poorer your ability to communicate the more likely you'll face ongoing situations which trigger each of you in this way. Let me give you an example of a common situation.

Many states explicitly promote the post-separation value of what is sometimes termed *first refusal.* First refusal means that when your child is with you and you can't directly parent him or her (for example if you get called in to work when you hadn't planned to have to work a shift), the other parent should get first refusal to pick up that parenting time. Cooperative parents who have established effective communication and who aren't using time with the child as a way of winning against each other will contact the each other in this situation and modify the parenting time that day so that the other parent can spend a few extra hours with the child. However, it often doesn't happen that way. For a variety of reasons (some more valid than others), parents will often not call the other parent to spend time with the child and, instead, get someone else to hang out with him or her.

When this type of thing happens, I hear all sorts of reasoning behind it. *He never seems to want to spend any time with her, anyway. She didn't allow me to make up the time I gave her last month so, I'll be damned if I give her any extra time, today!* It doesn't matter. The parent who would like to be offered first refusal simply won't see your point of view and agree with you. I'm not saying here that there aren't valid reasons to make the choice to not offer first refusal. The point is that perceiving the other parent as undermining your time or your relationship with your child is extremely triggering. It fuels ongoing hostility. It prevents cooperative behavior. It makes it more likely that parents will get locked into battles over small details of the parenting time schedule, or other aspects of shared parenting.

Another common issue is a parent perceiving the other parent as interfering with attempts to talk to the child on the phone. Countless parents have complained to me, *When I try to call, it goes straight to voice mail and she/he won't call me back.* Again, it doesn't matter what the explanation is for choosing not to communicate. It doesn't matter if it is a valid or invalid reason. The parent who perceives this behavior as getting between them and their child will go up a notch from *Code Orange* to *Code Red*. Count on it.

Do understand that I am not trying to convince you to *only* pay attention to this issue. Your goal is not merely to keep your other parent from ever thinking this way. But, the sets of parents who are the most successful at crafting a functional co-parenting relationship are the ones who cause this trigger less of the time.

Parents who ignore this issue are often exclusively focused on the reason for the behavior. *Of course I'm not answering the phone. He's a jerk and always starts a fight!* Or, *Dropping the kids off at her house would mean driving an extra fifteen minutes out of my way. My sister lives just next door.* I know that you have already, or will soon, experience this particular trigger. And, I assume it is one of the bigger triggers you have to deal with relating to your ex's behavior. Well, use your big brain and know that your ex have this same type of reaction to this issue. Ignore it and you'll open yourself to some lasting and unnecessary hostility.

# 5 HANDLING CHALLENGING EMOTIONS

Strong emotions are part of divorce. They likely became strong and challenging long before you separated. They remain strong for months or, even, years. They get triggered when you interact with the other parent. Many parents wish for an *off* button to avoid the distress of challenging emotions and to try to keep them from derailing interactions. Sometimes this results in strategies which come at risks and costs, such as drinking more. However, there is no *off* button. And, if there were, I'm not sure pushing it would be a good idea. So, *Plan B* is to deal with emotions constructively.

This chapter will discuss the common emotions of sadness and anger which are distressing and get in the way of functional co-parenting. You need to deal appropriately with these emotions so that they don't get in the way of your being a good parent and co-parent. Emotions are not entirely under your control, but you can choose when and how you react to your emotions.

It is important to think about emotions as functioning in the same way as stress. Strong emotions also influence our perceptions and thinking. Being aware of that can help you keep perspective and stay more in control of your reactions with your children and the other parent.

*Sadness*

Sadness is a common emotion of the grief process. Sadness is a normal response to the losses and changes that have happened and are happening. There may be particular thoughts that trigger sadness. Or, you may have a vague, but strong, sense of sadness, even when you aren't thinking about particular things that have changed. You may feel sadness as a form of empathy for your child's adjustments.

Sadness is not something your other parent needs to take care of. Your children are not responsible for taking care of your sadness, either. Certainly your ex and your children, and other people in your life, know when you are sad. But, you are the one responsible for your happiness. When you and your ex were together, you shared emotional closeness. That connection formerly meant that you shared emotions openly. And, you may have reasonably expected him or her to be emotionally supportive when you were feeling sad. Now you are renegotiating new boundaries. This includes no longer being as open with each other. It means not relying on each other to take care of our ongoing emotional status. Support for your sadness is best sought in other friendships.

If your sadness seems to be getting in the way of your functioning, seek competent therapeutic evaluation and care. Surely you will think, some of the time, that your sadness is related to the behaviors of your ex. However, as I discussed in the previous chapter, much of this type of thinking relates to the past. It has little positive function in the present. Sadness does not mean that you or your ex have done something wrong. An ideal separation between two very functional people will include some sadness.

One pitfall of feeling strong, challenging emotions is that they confuse our understanding of consequences and intentions. That is, we often attribute negative intentions on someone when that person's behavior results in negative consequences for us. This is not only true of events that lead to sadness, but all sorts of challenging experiences. For example, imagine that our daughter is with her mother one weekend. On that Saturday, her mother gets called in to work. While we generally call on each other to pick up some extra parenting time in this type of situation, she chooses to drop our daughter off at the grandparents' house for a visit. I could feel sad that I didn't get some extra time with our daughter. The sadness is the emotional consequence of the situation. I could attribute negative intentions on her mother by thinking, *She doesn't value my relationship with our daughter*, or, *She is doing things to keep our daughter away from me.* Any number of negative thoughts could arise. We do this. We equate consequences with intentions. But, often, we are wrong. And, even when we are partially accurate, we tend to have a negative bias because of this effect. Things get a negative spin. This is because many negative consequences have nothing to do with another person intentionally working to our disadvantage. But, we attribute intentions this way. Be vigilant for this effect.

## Guilt

Sometimes a parent is filled with the emotion of guilt after separation. This can happen for many reasons. One common reason is if the marriage ended because of an affair. In that case, one parent is usually wracked with guilt while the other is filled with strong anger. Or, a parent may feel guilty because they think they failed in some essential ways to keep the marriage alive. Whatever the thinking that underlies guilt, it can be a damaging emotion.

One way guilt can get in the way is in negotiations around post-separation agreements. These might be formal negotiations around property and family matters. Or they might be informal discussions of various co-parenting decisions. The guilty parent might choose to give up power in order to try to atone for their misdeeds or to just try to lower the tone of the anger from the other parent. I talked with an attorney recently who was celebrating this effect. He told me he loves it when one parent had an affair and he's representing the other parent, the angry one. He thinks this is a good situation because the guilty parent will give in on pretty much any issue without a fight.

That might be a good short-sighted strategy. To give in to atone for past bad actions. Or, to win because you were the victim of an affair. But, I don't believe it is a helpful dynamic for separated co-parents who both need to be collaboratively responsible for the ongoing parenting of their shared children.

I don't believe the long-term needs of a child are served by one parent always saying either *yes* or *no* in negotiations with the other parent. I certainly don't believe this should happen because of excess guilt or anger. A *yes* or *no* or a collaborative negotiation should be based as much as possible on the substance of the issue at hand.

If this is your situation, I recommend seeking individual, not joint, counseling to work through some of that emotion and put it into perspective. I strongly recommend that you be as conscious as possible of this dynamic in order to not have it dominate your co-parenting and to focus on the substance of issues rather than only your strong emotion.

*Anger*

Anger is a normal part of life. It is a normal part of grief. It happens in all relationships, including separated co-parenting. Each of us is involved in a long project of learning how to feel and express anger in functional ways and toward more desirable outcomes. We learn to deal with other's anger. When we each take our last breath, we'll still be working on this project.

Expect to be angry about your situation. Expect to get your anger triggered by your other parent. Feeling anger is not failure. The fact of anger isn't evidence of someone having done something wrong, through our brains often interpret it that way. Many parents wish for an off button for anger because it seems to be getting in the way of civil communication and collaboration. While you can shift toward a more cooperative relationship in which anger gets triggered less often, and to a lesser degree, I encourage you expect to be angry some of the time. Only hoping that it won't happen will leave you unprepared to deal with it effectively.

A lot can be said about anger. This chapter is just a jumping off point for experimenting with your own growth around feeling and expressing anger. And, there is much more to understand about anger than my advice here which focuses on anger in the context of separated co-parenting. I recommend that you read the book, *Letting Go of Anger: The Eleven Most Common Anger Styles & What to Do About Them* by Ronald and Patricia Potter-Efron. They discuss a variety of styles of anger and how to deal with each one. It can be useful to differentiate styles because you wouldn't make the same types of corrections with different people. For example, you wouldn't tell a person who stuffs her anger inside the same thing as a person who quickly gets very angry and explodes. You might also benefit from, *Angry All the Time: An Emergency Guide to Anger Control* by Ronald Potter-Efron. Both of these books will be very helpful if you already think that your anger skills need some work. But, even if you haven't been thinking this way, they will be particularly useful for you due to the consequences of not handling anger in your current situation.

The following sections of this chapter will focus on issues related to anger that have been helpful to parents with whom I've worked. These skills take some attention if you are going to get the benefits. Like many other strategies described in this book, you will need to experiment with them several times before they feel natural and begin to seem like they are working. Have faith.

*Be Aware of Your Anger*

It is essential to be aware of your anger if you are going to make careful and functional choices about how to deal with it. You may think this is strange advice if you, like so many parents, are often awash in anger. You may want much less awareness, not more, of your anger. However, I'm not suggesting you *be* more angry more of the time.

Awareness of anger helps you be aware of all levels of emotion. Being skilled at noticing lower levels of anger (we use words such as annoyed, or frustrated, for this) is helpful if it leads to more effective coping. It is easier to deal with frustration (say, level three on a scale of zero to ten) than being frankly pissed off (perhaps level eight for you). If you don't attend to the lower level and do something about it, you'll only react—internally and externally—when it is much more interfering. Perhaps at both levels, you may be thinking that another person is the source of your anger. But, reacting at a lower level makes it more likely you will be able to take responsibility for your reaction.

Be aware of how your express anger. How would I know that you are feeling angry if I were watching you in a challenging situation? How does your other parent know when you are angry? How do your children know? There are as many ways to express anger as there are people on the planet. We each have our individual style, even if there are typical elements of the ways that people express anger. Do you typically express anger in a way that serves you and others well? Have you expressed anger in an unhelpful way in past situations? Has your anger damaged a relationship before? While people at higher levels of emotional response often don't feel in control (this is because in that moment they often want to control the quality of their emotional experience and lack a sense of control because they can't), in fact you are making a series of choices when you react to your anger. What you say is your choice. What you do, including non-verbal behaviors, is under your control.

Be aware of the types of situations which result in your being angry. Different people have different triggers for angry. Some people remain cool in a situation that would enrage another. We are all unique in this way. What triggers you? You may discover that your stronger triggers happen when there is a lack of fairness in a situation, or when you feel disrespected, or when someone doesn't follow through with an agreement. Whatever your personal triggers, it is helpful to understand them.

If you have greater awareness of the type of situation that tends to trigger stronger anger, you can explore ways to work with it. For example, if you are a person who gets angry when others don't seem to follow through with agreements, you can explore how you can best support less triggering outcomes. You might focus on being a good communicator so there are fewer misunderstandings about agreements. You might examine how rigid or flexible you are about how you evaluate whether someone is following through or not. You might sometimes put a back-up plan in place so the other person's lack of follow-through is less problematic. There might be other strategies to deal with this. The point is that we each can take responsibility for having the type of experience we want to be having. We are not in total control of all aspects of our experience. We certainly aren't in control of others and only influence them part of the time to some degree. But, we are in control of what we pay attention to and how we choose to react.

In addition to identifying your stronger triggering situations, be aware of the context of emotional reactions. By this I mean that the particulars of a situation are often not the only factors which influence how we experience and react to emotions. Be aware of your stress level and how it influences your emotional reaction. Be aware of the relationship between sleep quality on a previous night, or in general, and emotional responses. Be aware of the influence of drugs or alcohol on emotions. There might be other factors you notice in your situation that influence the magnitude or quality of emotions. Developing this type of awareness makes it more likely you will put your emotional reaction into context. You will feel less out of control. Some of the time, you can make choices to manage those other factors when you have to deal with a triggering situation in order to dial out their interference.

Emotional expressions sometimes interfere with other messages we want to communicate. Awareness of anger can help you steer out of pure emotion and keep you focused on the issue at hand. In most co-parenting interactions, you probably aren't only wanting your other parent to know how angry you are. You often want him/her to understand something important. Or, you are negotiating with them around some issue. You want to persuade them to do something in a particular way. If the main, or only, message that you get across is that you are angry, you undermine your effectiveness at negotiating shared parenting.

*Identify the Should*

For most of us, most of the time, there is a reason we are angry. I'm not suggesting it's always a *good* reason. But, typically there is some logic to how and why we were triggered. At first, this may seem like silly advice. Of course, you know why you're angry. *She was late, again! He bad-mouthed me in front of the kids!* It's true that we often know why we are angry. So, why think about that, at all?

When we are angry, there is typically a *should* that provided the trigger. Sometimes there are multiple *shoulds*. You can understand it like this: If I am waiting in a parking lot for my other parent to meet me and my child and she is twenty minutes late, I might get angry. If I think about it, my anger is related to my judgments, *She should not be late*, and, *If she is going to be more than a few minutes late, she should call me.* It is those two *shoulds* that lead to my being angry, not her behavior.

If you're like a lot of people, you might want to argue with me. You might want to say, *No. The thinking didn't lead to the anger, her behavior did. The proof is that I wouldn't have been angry if she would have been on time.* Well, that may have been the case. But, it really was your thinking that led to your behavior. Remember the discussion in chapter five about levels of response. In one objective situation (she is late), there are many possible subjective responses (attachment, judgment, complaining, objectivity, creativity, acceptance, gratitude, or others).

Let me give you another example to illustrate the role of the *should*. Some parents think their children should clean their plate at dinner and some don't. Imagine a child, when eating with the family as guests at the house of someone special, leaves about twenty percent of their dinner on their plate at the end of the meal. The frustration level in the parent will be directly related to whether the parent has the plate-cleaning should or not.

I'm not suggesting that we try to never get angry by simply having no *shoulds*. This is impossible and undesirable. Even though many personal beliefs lead us to emotional triggers, on examination, we will likely decide that we want to keep them. I think people should, generally, treat each other in a fair manner. I think violence against vulnerable members of our society, including children, should be stopped. I'm not open to being persuaded to drop either of those *shoulds*. However, sometimes we have unreasonable *shoulds* which set us up for getting triggered. Most, if not all, of us are operating with some beliefs about the world that could, at times, be more flexible and result in fewer triggers.

If you are repeatedly getting angry about the same type of situation, it may be useful to identify your *shoulds*. Their not always at the front of your mind, but usually easily accessible if you think about the situation for a minute. Get out a notebook and write down one, or more, *shoulds* related to a recent situation in which you became angry. Let's go back to one of my examples. Imagine my other parent is late. Also, imagine that this is the only time she has been late over the last ten times we have met to exchange our daughter. So, if I become angry, it would result from thinking like this, *She should be on time every time we agree to meet and never late.* If I were to replace this thinking with, *Sometimes everybody has something come up that will make them late. She is generally very reliable and punctual,* then I won't get as frustrated. When we identify a belief that can be made more flexible in an acceptable way, then we can experiment with remembering it in that type of triggering situation. This is a good use of your therapist and I'll suggest two resources to explore this type shifting of thinking on your own: *Mind over Mood: Change How You Feel by Changing How You Think* by Dennis Greenberger and Christine Padesky and *How to Keep People from Pushing Your Buttons* by Albert Ellis.

When our *should* has to do with another person as in, *He should do this*, or, *She should do that*, we can examine whether we are best supporting the other person in conforming with our expectation. I have worked with many parents who have had triggering *shoulds* which they had never clarified and communicated explicitly. Many expectations seem so reasonable in our own heads, that we leave them unstated. The lack of clear communication, even around something you think can be left unsaid, increases the possibility that the other parent won't behave the way we want. I also suggest that you take stock of your behavior. Are you doing things that interfere with your expectations. I spoke with a couple recently who had a mutual expectation that each would call the other when there was something important happening with their shared child. It was also true that, most of the time, they descended into hostile arguing on the phone. Neither parent was enthusiastic about making such a phone call, unless they were prepared to face an unpleasant argument. They realized that they needed to change the arguing behavior in order to have the open phone calls take place.

Understanding the role of your thinking in the magnitude and quality of your emotional response can be empowering. When we think that someone else is making us angry, that thinking puts the source of our anger out of our control. When we understand our reaction as a result of the combination of their behavior and our thinking, then we may have less of a sense of being out of control. This will be true, even if we don't change the specific thinking that is leading to our emotional reaction. There is a big difference between, *When you do that, you make me mad*, and, *When you do that, I get mad*. It's a step toward emotional responsibility.

*Avoid Sarcasm*

Sarcasm is a common way that people express frustration with each other. Some people have a sarcastic style and express their thoughts about things, generally, in this manner. Some relationships are fraught with sarcasm. I caution you from employing sarcasm directly to your other parent or when speaking about the other parent to, or in front of, your child. Separated parents tend to have an overabundance of anger and share much more of it between them than is useful. Most of the time when you are feeling angry, nobody will benefit from your sharing it. Sorry about that, since you will often *want* to share it. Sarcasm increases the perception of others that you are angry. And, when it *is* appropriate to share anger, I believe that is best done with very low-level responses such as saying (only one notch, not two, above your normal calm voice), *I'm getting frustrated with this situation...* Sarcasm increases the perception of the magnitude of your anger—usually over the level that is useful.

Sarcasm delivers anger to your children that they don't deserve. They feel it as an attack since it is in response to one of their parents. And, they feel badly, even if they happen to be angry at the other parent for the same reason that you are. I spoke with a father one time who shared one child with his ex-wife. The mother was frequently very late to parenting time transitions and, occasionally, she wouldn't show up at all. The young child would often be very disappointed when this happened. The father's response was to say to the child in a very sarcastic tone, *Well, you know how she is.* When I confronted him about this, he did exactly what I expected. First he told me he was just stating "the truth". Then he told me he had a "very open" relationship with his child. To me, it didn't matter whether it was true. It was a type of openness that I do not see as nurturing. His sarcasm was mostly an expression of his contempt for the mother. However objectionable her actions, the child needed comforting, not to feel attacked. Children feel attacked when they hear one of their parents being attacked. You, as an adult would *take it personally* if I said something about one of your parents. It's no less true for your children. Regardless of whether you think sarcasm is cute, part of your style, or just a way of sharing humor, dial it out of your interactions with your other parent and your children.

*The Other Parent's Emotions*

An essential element of emotional skill is handling other's emotions. Simply hoping that strong emotion won't get in the way is not sufficient. And, thinking that your other parent shouldn't be feeling or expressing emotion won't work. It will happen. The best of parents will feel strong emotion some of the time when interacting.

Strong emotions aren't evidence of failure, but handling them poorly will lead to less desirable outcomes.

*Dealing with the Other Parent's Sadness*

Sadness is a normal part of separation. Sadness begins when each of you begin to realize the changes in your life, even before your actual separation. It is strongest during the separation and through the period of renegotiating your relationship boundaries. It tends to be most strong for the one who wanted the separation the least or who is most strongly identifying with the past. Sadness is always a feature of separation, though many people transmute their sadness into anger, which makes it less evident during interactions.

It is not your responsibility to fix your other parent's sadness. This is especially true of their sadness about the failed relationship. When you were together, you shared emotional openness, but this is one way you are now renegotiating your relationship. The loss of emotional connection can be one of the triggers for sadness. But, whatever the source of sadness for your other parent, she or he must seek other supports (such as friends, a therapist, or a pastor). You no longer function in that way.

While it is no longer your role to engage directly with your other parent's sadness, don't ignore it. Their sadness is a concern of yours to the extent that it is relevant to your co-parenting relationship. Let me give you an example. I spoke with a set of separated parents recently who needed to deal with the strong sadness of the ex-wife. They shared a very young child, so needed to have fairly frequent interactions around his care. When together, the mother was so sad about the divorce, she had difficulty not crying. Being together as the family that she had hoped would continue was highly triggering for her. They both saw this as undesirable, especially for their child who was just old enough to be able to notice this grief reaction. So, they negotiated ways to set up the exchanges of the child with minimal interactions in order to trigger the mother less. The mother also sought counseling to get support with her emotional response.

Another frequent form of post-separation sadness is triggered by lack of contact from children. Certainly, children miss their parents when they are separated from them, even if only for a few days. And, we parents miss our children when we don't have contact. While this is a normal part of separation, it can be interfering. This type of sadness on the part of the parent can be a problem when custody and parenting time schedules are being negotiated soon after separation. In an ideal situation, parents will wait to formalize their parenting schedule until everyone has had some weeks, or even months, to adjust to this issue. Perhaps there are issues of timing which warrant making a scheduling decision earlier. But, I have noticed that this adjustment to not being with children can be a strong motivator for parents to engage in some complicated battling over the schedule. Most parents find the initial periods of separation from their children challenging. This is normal. And, it is a part of separating a family. This may never totally go away. Parents who have been separated for a longer time may still miss their children when they aren't there and long for more parenting time. But, in the initial phase of separation, this feeling tends to be quite strong. I see it play into conflicts over the schedule quite frequently. There's no way to avoid these feelings. But, have some compassion for your other parent. Know that they are feeling this, too. And, when possible, put off formalizing your parenting time schedule until this early phase of more extreme missing of your child can subside somewhat.

## Don't Ignore the Other Parent's Anger

You might, at times, want to just not experience the anger of your other parent. You might wish you could cut it out, like the brown part of the banana. It's unpalatable. You don't like it. It gets in the way. And, it's worth paying attention to.

Often separated parents seem generally angry with each other, no matter what the circumstances. You might see your other parent as angry with you, no matter what you do. So, you might decide that your behavior no longer matters. But, it does matter. Even if you expect an angry response, you should steer your behavior toward that which will best support your children's needs, and which will make a workable co-parenting relationship more likely. As, I have explained in the early part of this book, even if your ex is trying to improve his or her behavior, it will be had to see that in the near future. So, throwing good judgment out the window is a bad idea. No one thing you, or your ex, will do will solve all the complications and lower the emotional level of your interactions. Some things may help a lot, but know that you will have to deal with a lot of complication and negativity for some time. It's not OK to decide that you can be as much of a jerk as you want simply because your ex will be pissed at you, no matter what. Behave with integrity, even if you are not currently expecting the reward. This will save your children a lot of stress. And, it may pay off in a positive way, later.

You both are going through a stressful and complicated period of adjustment. High emotions are normal, even when people are coping relatively well. These emotions will often be highly focused on each other. Expect it. It's normal.

If your other parent is experiencing and expressing anger in damaging ways that don't support effective negotiating or communicating, you should increase the structure. Have less live interactions. Have more limited contact. Limit, or eliminate, your contact when your children are present. This could include having a third party participate in exchanges of your children in order to limit face-to-face contact. Use e-mail rather than the phone.

One of the most challenging parts of dealing with anger is learning to be the target of anger. I'm not talking about being the target of abuse. I mean that some of the time people express anger toward us. Often when other people are angry with us, it is because something extremely important is going on in their head. They are triggered. And, it can be very useful for us to think carefully about why they are triggered. If you dismiss your other parent simply because they are always angry, you may miss something that is worth thinking about. This is a difficult thing that I'm suggesting. When others express anger toward us, we naturally get defensive. We focus on our side of the experience and discount whatever is going on over on the other side. We also just want it to stop and go away. But, when you are angry with your other parent, I expect that you often think it's about something you wish she or he would pay attention to, carefully. This will be true on the other side, too. However little you think they deserve your careful attention, you—and your children—are best served by your tracking why your other parent is angry.

It is also important to generally track the emotional level of your other parent. For example, imagine that I thought of an important issue to discuss with my daughter's mother. I plan to bring it up as soon as I see her. However, when I encounter her, she seemed highly stressed. She says, *I just had a really bad day at work*. If I discount her current emotional state and plow ahead with my issue, I'm probably not going to get an optimal result. Imagine that I'm angry with her. Imagine that I don't really care if she had a good or bad day. If I discount her emotional state, I'm about to start an argument in front of our child that would be best avoided until later. If you don't think your ex deserves your careful attention, your children certainly do.

*Ignore the Other Parent's Anger*

Now I'm going to give you the opposite advice. While it is prudent to track your other parent's emotional level and think carefully about why they may be feeling a particular quality of emotion, it can be calming to your interactions if you become less reactive. Your ex likely expresses anger toward you frequently. In those interactions, you two can spiral into conflict due to the emotion, regardless of the content. Even subtle, non-verbal, expressions of frustration can be enough to derail an interaction. Someone can roll their eyes, or let out a big sigh, and things are already headed downhill.

You are not in control of your other parent's emotions. And, your behavior does have an influence on their reactions. Perhaps your remaining calm in the middle of a conflict won't prevent them from getting irate. But, your becoming hostile will only make things worse. Certainly, it's easy to not care so much about this. You might think, in those moments, that they don't deserve your good behavior because they are behaving so badly. But, this isn't about what they deserve. It's about your responsibility to your children.

If this hasn't ever happened to you, I'm sure you've witnessed a time when two people were having some sort of conflict and one person remained relatively calm. It has an effect on the tone of the interaction. Even a separate person, less involved, who remains calm near two people arguing can keep the tone down. I think this is often part of the reason couples benefit from therapy. When parents fight in my office, they have me sitting a few feet away, remaining calm. This influences the tone of their conflict. If they were having the same conflict out of my office without my presence, they might escalate into a higher level of conflict.

In the previous section, I recommended thinking carefully about why your other parent is triggered. I maintain that as it can lead to your discerning helpful information about their current emotional state and what might be important to them. However, you will be well served to practice detachment from their expressions of anger. Notice them, but dial down your reaction as much as possible. Your adding more anger will not be helpful. And, your remaining more calm might help steer the interaction in a positive direction.

In tense interactions, you might think all sorts of nasty thoughts. You might have strong emotions. But, keep them to yourself. This might be a good moment to experiment with the time-out strategy discussed earlier. If one, or both, of you is highly triggered, it's a good time to ask if the building is on fire. If it isn't, stop the interaction and come back to it later. Or, pursue it in a non-live forum, such as e-mail.

I have interacted with more than five thousand separated parents and talked to many adults whose parents divorced with they were young. I have yet to hear a single person say, *That divorce would have been better if more anger would have been shared.* It's always the opposite.

Do your part, even when the other parent doesn't seem to.

*Be Trustworthy*

When relationships end, there tends to be a lack of civil, effective communication. There tends to be little collaboration because we tend to not collaborate closely with someone when we have a lot of negative emotions and unresolved conflicts. And, there tends to be very little trust. Trust often plummets to the basement near the end of a relationship. Perhaps the relationship ended due to a violation of trust. But, even if that wasn't the central issue, separated parents often interact in ways that damage trust. However, trust is essential for a workable co-parenting relationship. Being perceived as untrustworthy is a factor in emotional triggering.

Communication and collaborative conflict patterns are more readily improved than trust. You might choose to begin employing more civil communication and dealing with the other parent in a more collaborative way today and immediately start seeing positive effects. However, building trust takes time. Trust does not return with the same speed with which it left. This is part of the explanation for the continued, high emotional triggering during co-parenting interactions. This emotional level will subside when trust increases.

Being trustworthy in the co-parenting relationship means following through with agreements. It also means holding up your end of parenting responsibilities. You wouldn't want to leave your child with a babysitter whom you couldn't trust. This is no less important with you and your other parent. Each of you needs to be assured that the other parent is trustworthy.

Trust is a tricky thing to build. When it has eroded, it comes back slowly, if at all. Past violations of trust, especially ones that had consequences for your children can interfere with current trustworthiness. Failures to collaborate after separation can further complicate trust.

Do know that people who have violated trust in the past can be trustworthy now and in the future. If your ex had an affair and violated your trust, the hurt associated with that violation can powerfully affect your ability to trust them in any way. But, while this type of betrayal is lasting and often clouds the ability of two people to focus merely on co-parenting, it doesn't mean there will never be trust as co-parents. And, people who are not fully trustworthy in other areas of life may be able to develop trustworthiness in the co-parenting relationship.

Certainly, we often understand trust as an element of character. When someone expresses trustworthiness, their relationships are trusting. People can count on them. And, a lack of trust during separation is often seen as a character flaw. This may be objectively true. An outside observer might evaluate your other parent and decide that they generally are not trustworthy. However, I want to caution the overuse of this type of diagnosis.

The high conflict and turbulence through the end of the relationship means that parents will lose trust. This will happen even with generally trustworthy people. Remember that your brain is wired to look for confirming information when it has adopted a negative frame of reference. This also happens around trust. Some parents manage to navigate the end of the relationship with significant trust intact. But, many don't. The inability of parents to cooperate and be civil through the separation process violates trust. Trust also is eroded because of the issue with the green slice. Even if a parent *is* trustworthy, this information is clouded by high stress and unresolved conflicts. People may exhibit some of their most dysfunctional behaviors during a divorce. And, those behaviors will be magnified so that they seem even more dysfunctional.

I'm not suggesting that your lack of trust is completely misguided or that you should trust the other parent simply because of your having skewed perceptions. It would be unwise to place trust in someone in a way that sets you up for more violations. This would only lead in the opposite direction of where you want to go. I think you should only place trust in someone when it is prudent to do so, especially around issues that concern your children. But, you do need to be trustworthy in your agreements and co-parenting responsibilities. You also need to identify how your other parent is being trustworthy. And, you need to hold them accountable for being trustworthy. I'll discuss each in turn.

Try to not agree to something if you do not intend to follow through with the agreement. If you agree and then change your mind, notify the other parent. I know that this will be difficult for those of you who don't yet have a reliable method of clear communication in place and for those whose primary conflict style is avoidance. But, it is very important.

Each time the other parent experiences your not following through with an agreement, trust is eroded. It not only erodes trust around that particular issue, but in general. This may be more damaging for more consequential agreements, but it matters for small issues as well. Being chronically late for agreed transition times will result in the other parent feeling disrespected and not trusting. And, he or she will generalize that feeling so that it is not merely limited to transition time agreements. His or her brain will use this information as proof that you are generally untrustworthy. It will be one more bit of evidence to confirm that you are evil, stupid, and crazy. It erodes the co-parenting relationship and creates a rift that becomes difficult to repair.

When you fail to follow through with an agreement, acknowledge it. *I know that we agreed to meet at 6:00 and I am now thirty minutes late. I agree to make an effort to be on time after this.* But, don't make such statements if you don't have the will or capacity to follow through. A hollow promise with no follow through is just as bad. It undermines trust. I'm not a fan of apologies unless they are sincere and the person actually avoids doing the same thing again. Apologies are not very soothing when they don't mean that something actually will change for the better. Apologies with no follow-through make future apologies meaningless and annoying.

Being trustworthy by following through with agreements is part of my definition of being respectful. It is likely part of your other parent's sense of being respected, too. While you may not currently be feeling highly respectful of the other parent, it is important that you behave in a respectful manner. A parent discussed this issue with me a few days ago. He told me, *I hate my ex-wife. I hate her more than I have ever hated anyone. She can never, ever earn my respect, no matter what she does.* He told me she had cheated on him and then exploited him out of a lot of money before leaving. It is understandable that he feels betrayed and not genuinely friendly or trusting. Given his story of their relationship, I think he would be unwise to trust her as an intimate partner. And, they share a child. This father needs for his ex-wife to trust him as the co-parent of their child. He needs her to not worry that she can rely on him to hold up his end of the co-parenting relationship. If they didn't share a child, he could be as hostile and untrustworthy as he would want. But, his actions will have an impact on their evolving co-parenting relationship.

However undeserving of trust or respect he might view her, he will compromise a workable co-parenting relationship if he delivers his anger to her by flaking out on agreements. If he does so, each time he is untrustworthy, he is not only annoying his ex-wife (perhaps his short-term goal), but being an irresponsible parent (not the long-term goal). Responsibility as a separated parent means dealing with the other parent in a way that makes it more likely you can have a workable co-parenting relationship. Negative actions toward the other parent are negative actions against your children. Not all of that will be under your control. But, much of it is. You don't have to feel respectful, but you must behave in a respectful manner. You respect your children so, try to do this.

The validity of requests you have for your other parent to be trustworthy are made weaker by your own lack of trustworthiness. Some of that may be a matter of perception. The other parent may not be feeling trusting or respectful toward you and it may not have to do with your recent behavior. Things in the past can create lasting damages to relationships. But, you will make it more likely that your requests for follow-through will be taken seriously if you are doing an effort to do so yourself.

Much of your thinking about trustworthiness is probably focused on how your other parent *isn't* trustworthy. This is normal. And, your perceptions are influenced by those brain effects I have described in the early part of the book. Unfortunately, you are wired to not see when your other parent *is* trustworthy. This is part of that issue with missing the green slice. No parent I've worked with has been completely untrustworthy although, many have been quite untrustworthy in ways that really mattered. I'm not trivializing those issues. But, most parents are being trustworthy in some ways. However, those things get obscured by the triggering issues. However challenging it might be, I recommend that you contemplate your other parent's behavior. Identify how they *do* follow through with agreements, even if they often don't. There are some ways you can rely on them as your child's other parent. If you think this is totally not true in this moment, be open to seeing it if it does materialize in your situation. Not seeing it, when it is actually there, is to miss the green slice.

## Don't Attack Your Child When Triggered by the Other Parent

Parents often commit what I call an *attack by proxy*. That is, they get angered about something having to do with the other parent, but the parent is not there. The child is the one present and who gets to be the target of the anger. Parents who do this often justify it by maintaining that it isn't an attack on the child since they are triggered by the other parent, not the child. But, I maintain, it is an attack on the child because: 1) it's an expression of anger and the child is the one present to get the full energy of the negative emotion and, 2) the child feels it as a personal attack against them; they take attacks on family members as attacks on them directly.

If you don't buy this, imagine that you and I were going to travel one hour to a nearby city in your car. It so happens that your current girlfriend/boyfriend handles advertising contracts for my business. Five minutes before we were to leave, I got a bill from your current partner which I believe grossly overcharges me for recent services. I was unable to reach her/him on the phone. So, for the entire car trip, I rant angrily to you about how much I hate her/him. Will this be unpleasant for you? Will you, potentially, take it personally because it's someone you love and are close to? Will you feel helpless to stop it since you can't fix the business problem? Or will you feel completely neutral thinking, *Oh, that's not about me, it's about my girlfriend/boyfriend?* Children experience attacks on a parent as an attack on them. We all do. It's why others have no right to bad mouth our parents. We take it personally. Let me give you another example.

I worked in a case one time in which the parents shared a nine-year old boy who was significantly overweight. Both parents were concerned about the son's weight, but the father's way of dealing with it was to call the son *fat* and make him eat salad, and only salad, all weekend while he ate whatever he wanted. When he would return to his mom's house, his mom would ask him how his weekend went. The son would say, *Not very much fun…Dad called me fat and made me only eat salad.* The mom, angered by this, said to the son, *Of course your dad will say stupid shit like that. He is not loving. That's why I divorced him.*

I believe the mom had good intentions of being supportive of the son. She wanted to name the bad behavior. And, she was reasonably angry hearing that the dad acted that way. But, what she did was commit an attack by proxy. The dad wasn't present when she got triggered. And, so she dumped her anger on the son. However problematic the behavior, an attack on a parent is felt, by the child, as an attack on them. What the son effectively heard was, *You are stupid. You are not loving. I might divorce you if I don't like you.* I don't believe the mom's actions did what her intentions set out to do. Imagine the difference from the son's perspective if the mom had felt the anger, caught herself before reacting negatively, remembering the need to support the son, and said, *I'm sorry you had a bad weekend, I really am. I'm sure it wouldn't feel good for anyone to call you fat, especially your father. I can't control what he does, but I'll agree to talk to him about this.*

I believe if the mom had said this latter statement, her words would have done what she intended. The son was sad and needed support. He didn't need to be the target of anger.

You will get your anger triggered by the other parent when only your child is present. As challenging as it may seem, stifle it. Don't react until you can at least be neutral. If, in that moment, you are too angered to possibly say something better, say nothing at all. If you are reacting non-verbally with extreme tension, leave the room. Give yourself a time-out. Interact with the child when you have calmed down and *still* don't say negative things about the other parent.

It is more acceptable to say, *I don't agree with what he said*, or, *I'm not sure what to think about that, let's talk about it later*, or deal with the child's emotions without focusing on the other parent as in, *How are you feeling, are you OK?* But, it is not acceptable to attack the other parent's character as in, *She's always like that*, or, *She's lazy, no good, and just does things to get a rise out of me*, or, *Well, there he goes, again*!

I've talked with hundreds of adults whose parents divorced when they were children. I have yet to hear a single person say, *Boy, things would have been even better after the divorce if my mom had been more angry about my dad*, or, *I had a pretty good childhood, but I really wish my dad had been more open with me about how angry he was with my mom after the divorce*. It's always the opposite message. Spare your children, please.

*Fan the Flames, and You Will Get Burned*

It is common for children to have different relationships with each parent (as well as other caregivers). A child may be closer to and more emotionally open with one parent compared to the other. In general, this is not a problem to be fixed. Children experience this even when parents don't separate. I'm guessing that you would report that you have a different relationship with each of your parents.

So, children are commonly closer to one parent than the other. In some families the difference is greater than others. This is sometimes due to an early stage of development. Young children become more attached through play and direct parenting. If one parent has provided much more of the direct parenting to a young child, we would expect to see more attachment with that parent. In such a case, a much more even amount of attachment may emerge if the other parent has the opportunity to have more direct interactions. This greater opportunity may even be promoted by the parenting situation after separation. The parent to whom the child is less attached may have more interactions with the child after separation.

Another common post-separation issue is that of the child aligning with one parent in opposition to the other parent due to the child's perception that one parent is the good guy and the other the bad guy. The specific way that children tend to adopt this thinking is dependent on their stage of development (younger children have a more simplistic view of the life situations of adults than older children) and how they may have been exposed to their parents' conflicts (they may see the divorce as being the fault of one parent with the other parent being the victim).

Whatever the dynamics and underlying explanation, a child is likely more aligned with one parent than the other after divorce. And, this creates a pitfall to be avoided. The parent who is currently enjoying more alignment with the child may be tempted to exploit that alignment as a means of winning against the other parent. They may see the alignment as justification of trying to limit the other parent's parenting time. They may see fanning the flames of the child's hostility or resistance to the other parent as instrumental in winning a legal battle over custody or parenting time. Or, they may disregard their normal parental boundaries and treat the child as a peer, feeling free to talk badly about the other parent as though they were talking to a close friend.

So, in the short-term, the parent enjoying the child's alignment may see this as legally and instrumentally advantageous. I believe this is often the motivation for a parent to try to involve the child in the court proceedings. A parent is, understandably, more happy to have the child talk to the judge, or otherwise directly participate in the court proceedings, if he/she believes the child will say things that support the ultimate legal goal (most often a petition for primary physical custody or change of custody). This dynamic, putting the child in the middle by the parent who enjoys the more positive alignment, can last for years. Sometimes it is more subtle but mostly manifesting as that parent feeling free to say negative things to or in front of the child about the other parent. But, here is what often happens.

Your child wakes up each day with a brain more developed than the day before. As they develop, they are able to view the world through increasingly wise eyes. You can get by with saying outrageous things to a five-year old that an eight-year old won't buy. You can get by with things with the eight-year old that won't fly with a twelve-year old. Sooner or later (and usually sooner if the badmouthing parent is less restrained and often displays anger about and toward the other parent), your child will form the perception that your anger toward the other parent, and the way you have expressed it, has damaged his/her relationship with the other parent.

This emerging consciousness often happens as children approach puberty because developmentally they are at a stage where they begin to push against both parents for some new freedom. If they test that limit with the parent to whom they have been aligned and get resistance (which they should since both parent should actually be parenting partly by appropriately setting limits), they often begin to reassess that relationship. It can happen sooner. It can happen later. But, if a child has been hostile and resistant toward a parent and later has the perception that the parent to whom they were closer has been fanning the flames of their issues with the that parent, they will blame the parent to whom they have been close. This will happen even if the child is not totally accurate in their perceptions.

When they get old enough to have more discerning understandings of what goes into a quality relationship and they assess their relationship with the parent toward whom they've been hostile, they will eventually try to make sense of it. If they decide that the closer parent has set them up to be more hostile than they might have been, they will feel betrayed. Some children react to this sense of betrayal quite strongly. In some cases, I have seen the alignment of the child flip from one parent to the other. I have seen cases where the formerly close relationship was permanently damaged, or even ended. This sense of betrayal often takes years to resolve, if ever.

So, be neutral to positive when speaking to or around your child about the other parent. Even what you see as mild joking about the other parent (if understood later by your child as your having contributed to their problems with the other parent), can result in this sense of betrayal. When they are very young, they'll take your words at face value if they are aligned with you. But, every single day they get older and wiser and will eventually hold you accountable for what they might see as a set-up and betrayal.

# 6 BETTER COMMUNICATION 101

So, far, we have focused on how you experience and handle post-separation conflict. Your thoughts, influenced by predictable brain shifts influence how you react to interactions with the other parent. And, the words you use matter a lot. The earlier strategies mostly have to do with working with how you view your co-parenting relationship and shape your general process of interaction. In this chapter, I offer some ways to improve your communication skills to further dial out divorce stress and more effectively communicate. The strategy *Use Clean Language* will improve your communication with the other parent, but also your children. The remaining strategies pertain mostly to how you communicate with the other parent.

*Dial Up Structure: Use Live Communication Less*

You probably want a relationship with your other parent in which you can contact him or her whenever an important issue arises in order address it. And, you want those interactions to be civil and collaborative. But, many parents go through a phase after separation in which random encounters or contacts result in unsatisfying conflicts. The issue at hand doesn't get addressed and the experience of the interaction is unpleasant. This can be damaging to the process of building a constructive ongoing relationship. If it continues, it will delay the goal of collaborative co-parenting. One method for dialing out this negative influence of ongoing, unsatisfying conflicts is to add structure. Think about this. How strongly would you agree with the following statement?

> ***When we contact each other, we generally are able to discuss co-parenting issues without spiraling into unsatisfying conflict.***

If that doesn't describe you very well, you may want to dial up structure until it improves. I know that in the short-term, adding structure can get in the way of flexibility. Eventually, you may want to not impose too much structure in favor of more ad hoc communications. I support this. And, experimenting with more structure can be valuable method for achieving that goal, especially if part of what is getting in the way is a pattern of unsatisfying conflicts.

This strategy helps in two ways. First, when you are having less live (face-to-face or on the phone) and more non-live (e-mail, snail mail, or texting) interactions, you can be somewhat off the hook in terms of your less helpful patterns of spiraling into an unproductive argument. You can get a triggering e-mail and calm down before replying more easily than you can when you hear your other parent say something triggering in-person. If you get a triggering text and flip out, your other parent does not witness your reaction and only is aware of the civil, clear response you send after you've calmed down. Second, when you structure interactions, you can prepare for them before-hand, rather than feeling blind-sided by them. You can choose to not communicate in moments when you are not on top of your game, when you are too stressed out to effectively deal with the issue, or are distracted by some other issue.

Non-live communication also helps with accountability. A parent told me recently that she and her child's other parent were having an ongoing issue about not being on the same page with agreements. For example, they would have a conversation, in-person or on the phone, about the time for a transition. Then on the day of the transition, her other parent would often arrive at a different time than what she thought they agreed upon. They would then get into an argument (in front of their child) about the misunderstanding. At some point, they switched to only negotiating the parenting time schedule via e-mail. After switching to e-mail, this particular misunderstanding no longer occurred. They were each more clear about the schedule because they were literally typing it out to each other. And, they could go back and refer to the earlier e-mails if they weren't clear about the agreement. They went from having this type of argument almost once a week to not at all just by switching the discussion to e-mail.

I do understand that e-mail and texting also have issues. A parent complained recently that sometimes he and his other parent would get into conflicts because they were misinterpreting the tone of e-mails. E-mails lack a lot of aspects of communication that we often rely on in order to understand the meaning of the words. If I am standing in front of you, you will see my body language and hear things in my voice that you will not be able to see if I send the same words to you via e-mail or text. However, if live communications are regularly getting derailed, you should experiment with non-live (e-mail or snail mail) or less live (texting) for some time. And, I recommend that you send only limited e-mails or texts. By this I mean limit each communication to only one and not a bundle of issues. And, use as few words as possible. When I have parents bring in e-mails during the coaching process, I usually ask them to reduce long (two to five paragraph) e-mails to two or three sentences. Each additional, unnecessary, phrase or sentence is potentially triggering for the other parent. Be brief.

Another method for dialing up structure is to limit your interactions in time. One example of this is from a set of parents who worked with me recently. They had decided that for most co-parenting issues, they would meet briefly (for about 30 minutes) once each week while their child was at school. Because they did this regularly, each knew that if they thought of a relevant issue to the discuss, they could wait until that weekly meeting. Because they scheduled this meeting regularly, they could anticipate it and be prepared (mentally and emotionally) in advance. They reserved ad hoc communications for truly urgent issues (as in, our child is sick and needs to go to the doctor). The point is: *Don't interact every day if you don't have to.* Even if you have a reason to interact more often (for example, because your parenting time schedule changes frequently due to shifting work schedules), leave the non-urgent issues for the non-live portion of your communication pattern. If you practice structuring your communications this way, one thing that can happen is that you start to build trust. This is because a greater percentage of your interactions are neutral to positive. This is direction in which you should be heading. Structure is the method to get there.

Structured and limited communications also help during the renegotiation of your relationship boundaries. You experienced months or years of high intimacy and are now creating a lot of space between you. You are renegotiating your boundary of general involvement. This doesn't happen overnight. While communication is often considered the sharing of information, it is also a form of contact. Separated parents may be initiating communication in order to maintain a closer contact. That closeness was a feature of your former relationship. But, now sparse communication may be more appropriate. If you are initiating frequent communication with your other parent, be aware of how this pattern may look a lot like the way you communicated when you were together. Allow it to shift so that you focus on co-parenting tasks, not communicating to seek satisfying contact. If your other parent seems to be initiating frequent communication partly in order to maintain contact, know that this is normal. They may not be doing it in an acceptable way or frequency. You may want to shape the interactions toward a pattern that seems more appropriate to you. But, it is a normal issue to have to negotiate after separation.

*When Possible, Prepare Ahead of Time*

Have you ever noticed the difference between what is on your shopping list and what ends up in your cart when you get to the check-out? We careen through life largely guided by impulses. Some of the time this serves us better than others. In interactions with your other parent, acting impulsively will often be directly connected to swerving off-course. At least in until you craft a relatively workable and flexible co-parenting relationship characterized by little conflict, you should stick to delivering a simple message. And, when possible, you should think about that message ahead of time.

Imagine there is a triggering situation with your other parent. For example, she or he doesn't share information sent home from your child's school which sometimes keeps you out of the loop in terms of academic progress and the sports events in which your child participates. It's an ongoing issue and you feel angry about it. Two days ago another instance of this happened which resulted in your not knowing about your child's basketball game until after it had happened. This evening, you will see your other parent when you transition your child and you will have the opportunity to bring it up. You might tell me, *Jon, I am prepared. I know exactly what the issue is and how I feel about it. There's nothing to prepare.* I think there are two ways to prepare.

Assuming you have spent a few minutes thinking about how (face-to-face or via e-mail or whatever) and when (today, later, never) to bring this up, you can be more prepared if you anticipate that this will be a stressful interaction and you do something to lower your stress. This was discussed in the chapter on general stress. You can also think carefully about what you intend to try to accomplish in your communication. Do you want the other parent to hear your concern about the issue? Or, are you wanting to negotiate with him or her toward a specific resolution? Whatever your goal, what do you intend to say? How do you expect the other parent to react? Is there a way to communicate that better serves your goal?

*Be Brief: Avoid Communication Bundles*

Our big brains are capable to coming up with more information to share than is reasonable. When there are stretches of time between interactions with the other parent, your brain can create a rich list of issues to discuss when given the next opportunity. However, in most interactions, too many details will overwhelm your shared capacity to deal with them effectively. The strategy discussed in the prior section, preparing ahead of time, is one antidote to this potential pitfall. To the extent that you are conscious of the various issues you *could* bring up, you can choose to focus on those which are more important and urgent, leaving the others for another time.

Another version of this issue is impulsively adding on another issue, even if you carefully prepared to talk about the one on which you focused in the beginning of the conversation. Be deliberate. Be slow. If you think of something, try to think for a second or two before opening your mouth. If the other parent brings something up for which you are not prepared, consider its urgency factor *before* you react. If it isn't urgent (meaning you need to address it right now or someone will face less-desirable consequences), politely agree to address it in the near future. You and your other parent simply do not need to address all of the issues you can think of in the moments when you think of them. The best of us get overwhelmed when faced with too many issues to deal with. By sequentially focusing on one issue at a time, you can build some more successful experiences. If you don't edit in this way, you or the other parent will tend to load up your interactions with too much complexity which will have the opposite effect. Each interaction will be proof that the two of you can't co-parent effectively. Don't let bundling undermine the possibility of your feeling more hopeful about becoming more workable co-parents.

*Use Clean Language*

Clean language is the antidote to the pervasive, negative thought process that dominates the thinking of separated parents. The grief process, current stress, and unresolved conflicts add up to a very clouded view of reality. I have described this mode of thinking as: *This is hell because my ex is evil, stupid, and crazy*. Now, having talked to thousands of parents, I come to expect this. But, it is unhelpful because of the way it influences parents to swirl into more stress and co-parental conflict than necessary. It also makes it more likely that parents will talk to, or around, their children in ways that are damaging. I encourage you to be vigilant if your thinking is swirling into this unhelpful mode and practice clean language instead.

What I notice when interacting with parents who are either newly separated or still going through the (often months-long) period of adjustment is that the content of their experience is filtered through the powerful lens of the separation. During this highly stressful and emotionally charged period, it is difficult to *not* think of the separation and its consequences. So, all perceptions—even those which have little, or nothing, to do with the separation—will lead to this type of thinking. Someone comments, *It's a nice day, today*. And, you think, *I bet he's out on his boat…with his new girlfriend, dammit!* Or, your child asks about plans for her upcoming birthday party and you instantly are thinking about how awful it will be since there will be two parties, not one, as you and the other parent can't get along well-enough to be at the same party. Or, as I described in an earlier chapter, a daughter asking her father to buy a pair of jeans to which he responds, I would buy you the jeans, if your mother hadn't had all those affairs.

Certainly separation is a special type of hell. It is complicated and stressful. It challenges our sense of self and makes the difficult task of parenting even more complicated. While it may provide relief from some of the negative parts of your former relationship, it brings new issues. Parents are normal for being in a negative mode of thinking that is primarily focused on that stress. And, the complications and unresolved conflicts with the other parent, along with past affronts, do make it understandable that parents would focus on blaming the other one for that stress. I'm not saying you're crazy for thinking this way. I am saying you have a responsibility to your children to be conscious of how this thinking can get in the way of optimal parenting and workable co-parenting. To deliver the message of *this is all hell* to your child is unsettling, to put it mildly. To tell them that their other parent is evil, stupid, and crazy is damaging to them in two ways. First, they will feel attacked because it is *their* parent whom you are attacking. There is no way for them *not* to take this as a personal attack against them. Second, to attack them by saying nasty things about the other parent goes into their core and has lasting negative effects. Let me tell you a story to illustrate this.

An acquaintance of mine told me about losing her son, which happened a few years before I met her. She had two children and was closest to her younger son. One day, he took a trip with some friends. A few miles out of town, they had an automobile accident and he died. She told me that for a solid year she dropped into a deep depression. She couldn't accept his death. Her marriage suffered. Her relationship with her other child suffered. Her job suffered. Her life was miserable. One morning, about a year after his death, she was lying in bed. She apparently wasn't trying to think positively, but had some random epiphany. She suddenly remembered many times—going all the way back to her early childhood—when people had said positive things about women in her family.

She told me that she remembered people talking about her great-grandmother as being a strong and resilient woman after immigrating to the united states long ago. Members of her family had talked positively about her aunt as a strong and resilient woman when she had suffered cancer and went through surgery, chemotherapy, and radiation treatments. Her family talked about her mother as a strong and resilient woman when she was laid off and had to go back to school to train for a new career. She remembered times when people said these things to her, but also many times when it was just something she overheard, or even just a sense of the lore of her family.

Remembering those positive moments, she suddenly had a sense of strength and resilience. She told me that her grief didn't immediately go away. But, it was a turning point for her. She was able to begin healing and, eventually, returned to a more functional life. I think about this woman every time I talk to parents about using clean language. I firmly believe that if, instead of messages of strength and resilience, my friend had heard the awful things parents often say about each other to and around children during divorce, she wouldn't wake up with renewed strength. And, this effect was decades later after most of these comments.

You may have many moments when you are triggered and think your other parent is evil, stupid, and crazy. I will not argue with you about whether your anger is justified. Perhaps. And, I will not argue with you about whether it is true for you in that moment. Perhaps. However, I will caution you from using justified feelings and being right as permission to say these negative things to, or around, your child.

This type of negative language also undermines the quality of your co-parenting relationship. When a parent is aware of the other parent saying negative things to a shared child, even if the parent doesn't take the attack personally, it is seen as inadequate, or bad, parenting. It may seem that the attacking parent doesn't care about the emotional welfare of the child. Witnessing one's child attacked is probably more stressful than being attacked directly. This erodes trust. You have a responsibility to your child to avoid this type of attack. And, you must avoid it because of how it affects the perception of your other parent.

*Stop Complaining*

Complaining is not clear and effective communication. It creates resistance in the others with whom we are negotiating. If I had chosen in this book to complain about how many parents with whom

I have worked have been jerks, or have not followed through with my advice, or have made choices I didn't agree with, and had not focused on practical co-parenting strategies, you would have bailed on reading in the first chapter. Complaints are useful or pleasant. This is no less true between you and your other parent.

I'm a fan of Marshal Rosenberg's *Non-Violent Communication*. His method offers many useful strategies including his promoting delivering doable requests to other people. Instead of saying, *You're driving too fast*, you can request, *Please drive at, or below, the speed limit*. Instead of saying, Respect me!, you can say, Please don't interrupt me when I'm speaking. Instead of saying, Why don't you live up to your obligations?, you can say, I would like to you to arrange your schedule so you can take our son to ball practice, too.

When two people have unresolved conflicts, they usually communicate this in two ways. One is non-cooperation. They just don't do whatever the other person wants them to. This is a vague and unhelpful way to let someone know you don't like them, or something they did. The other way is through complaining. *I don't like this! I don't like that! You suck! You always sucked! You will always suck!* If it truly is your goal to improve your co-parenting relationship, complaining will not get you there. Cut it out. Complain to your friend or your brother (when your child is not present, even to overhear the complaint). Complain to your therapist. Complain in your private diary. Don't complain to your child or other parent.

Follow Rosenberg and deliver specific, doable requests. Think ahead of time about whether your request is specific and doable. Would an objective, outside observer understand what you mean and be able to easily evaluate whether the person complied with your request? I strongly urge you to check out Rosenberg's book, *Nonviolent Communication*, or workshops in NVC which can be easily found on the internet and may happen in your city.

*Avoid Universals: Be Specific*

Two parents were in my office, recently. One issue was that the father was often late to transitions. They were both in agreement that about ninety percent of the time, he was twenty to forty minutes late. He wasn't arguing with the mother about the details of how often or how late he was. But, later in the session, when the mother said, *You're always late!*, guess what he did? He immediately jumped to defend the ten percent of the times when he was on time. It took ten minutes for them to stop arguing about this.

This type of thing happens when we use universal statements, such as always or never. People get into (mostly useless and distracting) arguments trying to qualify them. So, avoid them when you can. The antidote to this problem is being specific. There is a difference between, *You never do the dishes!*, and, *It is your turn to do the dishes*, or, *You didn't do the dishes this time and it was your turn.* Being specific doesn't prevent conflict. You may still end up having to sort out your difference. But, using a universal will often lead to a useless level of conflict or down a tangent that ends up not solving the issue at hand.

*Use "and" instead of "but"*

Most of the time, when I notice sentences which include, *but*, I think that, *and*, would have served better. It serves better for the meaning and to reduce the level of conflict. Consider this scenario: two parents are having conflict over the location of parenting time transitions. One parent says, *Yes, you want to meet halfway but, I have to pick Johnny up from school those days.* As soon as but shows up in the sentence, it negates the value of what would have, otherwise, been a good strategy: validating the other parent's concern. This invalidation will reduce the other parent's sense of being heard, even though the first parent tried to include it in the sentence. This parent would have been better served to say something like, *Yes, you want to meet halfway and, I'm worrying about getting there on-time since I have to pick Johnny up from school those days.* When you use *and* instead of *but*, you keep both concerns on the table. You make it less likely that your other parent will think you're ignoring their concerns.

Using *and* is a helpful strategy if you are dealing with someone who uses *issue switching* during conflict. Issue switching is a strategy for diverting the focus of a conflict. Here's an example: You arrive home and your roommate didn't do the dishes. You say, *Hey, it was your turn to do the dishes this week.* Your roommate responds, *Well, you didn't take out the trash last week when it was your turn.* Issue switching is a way to say, I'm not listening to you, let's talk about my problem with you. A response to keep both issues on the table would be to say, *Yes, it's true that I didn't take out the trash last week, and, you haven't done the dishes this week.*

Consider employing *and* in some situations when you have an urge to use *but*. Catch yourself when you are issue switching since it tends to not address substantive content and may increase the level of conflict in your interaction or relationship.

*Communicate about Things that Matter to the Other Parent*

A common issue is the lack of sharing of consequential information between them about children. This sometimes takes the form of frustration due to not being notified of school-related events or academic progress reports. Sometimes it takes the form of frustration about a child's activities which require both parents to make scheduling arrangements, such as taking a child to a sports practice. It might take the form of frustration about expenses incurred due to a child getting medical services or being enrolled in some activity such as a school sport. Whatever the issue, consider communicating clearly with your other parent when your choices will impact him or her financially or otherwise.

Two excuses parents often give about why they don't communicate about these issues are, *Well, I have sole legal custody, so I don't have to consult him*, and, *If I try to communicate about this, we'll just get into a fight.* Let me address each of these.

If you have the legal right to make a unilateral decision, it doesn't mean that your other parent will like your decision or how you communicate about it. Your goal is not merely to act in congruence with court orders, but to move toward a more workable co-parenting relationship.

You might be thinking that you are in a bind. If you *don't* tell your other parent about something, say which pediatrician you have chosen, then she or he will be angry. If you *do* tell, then she or he will be angry because of wanting to make a different decision or having wanted to have legal custody her-/himself. You may have to deal with this aspect of the situation. And, it is still very important to practice a policy of informing your other parent about information that you would want to know yourself.

*Don't Communicate Through Your Child*

The fact that you and your other parent haven't yet developed a pattern of effective communication is not a good reason to communicate through your child. If you need a third party to deliver communications, choose someone other than your child. There are several reasons this is not good for you or your child.

When children are used as intermediaries, you suffer from their lack of development. You will be filtering your interactions through a juvenile brain. Bad idea! Imagine this scenario: Two parents are having trouble communicating, so they seek my advice which is: use a third person to deliver messages back and forth. These two parents don't immediately think of a good candidate and ask me to choose one for them. I think of two potential people, one a forty year-old and the other a ten year-old. Which one do you think would be better in that role? Why are you thinking that? I hope that you would select the forty year old because the ten year old is more likely to screw up the message. Adults talk in adult language and are better understood by adults. Whatever sweet qualities you think children have and bring to social interactions, they are simply too juvenile to competently handle complex and consequential information much of the time.

Parents routinely ignore this issue when using their children to deliver important information.

Your children need to get the message that your divorce and the resulting stress are not their fault. Communicating through them puts them in an active role when they should be passive or out of the loop, altogether. When conflicts arise as a result of communications passed through children, they will feel responsible. The details of complex negotiations are not their responsibility. The outcomes of your co-parenting choices are not their responsibility. You can maintain your appropriate responsibility and reduce your child's inappropriate sense of responsibility by not communicating through him or her.

When parents communicate, these messages are often heavily laden with emotion—usually anger. Your children need to be dealing with their own emotional reactions to the separation without your heaping your emotions on them. Even if your message is ultimately aimed at the other parent, your child will feel and react to the anger in it. And, it is not their job to deliver anger, or any other emotion, on your behalf. Putting them in that position creates emotional confusion for them.

Even when parents don't separate, children often play both ends against the middle in order to get their way. When parents are separated and don't communicate directly, children will still do this. And, in that situation, they will do it with greater consequences—for them, and you. Direct communication between parents is one way to hold children accountable for what they say and do. But, it only works if you actually have that line of communication open. Again, when this type of communication failure results in conflict between parents, the child will be caught in the middle.

Children, in the puberty or teen years, may initiate this type of behavior and parents can fall into unnecessary conflict if it isn't handled properly. A teen child might call one parent and say that the other parents asked them to say something. If that parent takes the message at face value, then the teen is being given too much power and it could produce conflict between the parents. When a teen calls and says, *Dad said...*, the appropriate response is, *OK. I'll talk to Dad about that.* If you assume the other parent really said whatever it was, you may get triggered. Now you're engaged in conflict with the other parent through your child. Don't do it.

*Talking to Your Child on the Phone*

One of the biggest sources of sadness for children and parents after separation is missing each other. A common issue that comes up for separated parents relates to talking to children when they are at the other parent's house. In general, phone calls between children and their parents helps alleviate this sadness and maintain the sense of connection. However, I hear about this issue often because it is not without difficulties.

Children under the age of three don't meaningfully participate in or benefit greatly from being on the phone. Perhaps it can be satisfying for the parent, but the child's cognitive development hasn't progressed enough for such calls to maintain or expand attachment as they will later.

Between the ages of three and puberty, phone calls can function to help the child maintain a sense of connection with the parent when they are in the custody of the other parent. This may be particularly helpful for younger children who have periods of separation from a parent of two or more days. Children ages three to five have a less-developed sense of time compared to older children which is why parenting time schedules for younger children are ideally arranged to avoid long periods between parenting transitions.

One problem that often arises is a child's lack of enthusiasm for being on the phone with a parent. Some children, by temperament, may enjoy talking on the phone. However, it is quite common that children won't initiate or get very richly involved in phone conversations with their parent. Of course, this is not very satisfying for the parent who misses the child and would prefer to have more contact. When the child refuses to participate in phone calls or only stays on the phone for very short periods of time, do not assume that the other parent is running interference. It could be the child. Parents often fight over this as though it is being done with malicious intent.

Certainly, parents should not interfere with reasonable phone contact. Withholding phone contact of the child with your other parent should only happen with just cause. I do believe this issue gets muddled due to the common practice of parents choosing to fight on the phone after the child has spoken with one parent. That behavior results in parents not supporting the child's calls. It also sours the experience for the child. Avoid that. Separate your calls from those of your child. I don't believe parents should get involved in phone conflict when children are present. So, if you are following that rule, then your child's calls will remain untainted.

Children in late puberty and into the teen years do not need constant contact to maintain connection. They have a much more developed and flexible sense of relationships and time. So, with older children, I strongly discourage fights between parents over routine, daily phone calls with the child. It is reasonable to negotiate this type of contact directly with the child if it can be done in a way that doesn't set the child up to have conflict with either parent or to be caught in the middle of parental conflict. If the child doesn't have the same enthusiasm as you about daily phone contact, drop it. It's a sad thing for you as a parent. But, it isn't worth the fight.

One situation in which I have recommended that parents experiment with limiting phone contact with the child is when the phone call precipitates a severely troubling episode for the child. Children report that one of the worst things about their parents' divorce is missing one parent all of the time. I have worked in several cases where a child becomes highly emotionally triggered from the phone call with the other parent due to missing them. The phone call sometimes results in hours of upset. This is most common with younger children. Sometimes limiting or avoiding the phone calls for a few weeks helps the child be more emotionally stable and adjust to the situation of separated homes.

## Have the PROCESS Conversation

People in relationships often talk *about* their relationship. Boyfriends, girlfriends, husbands, and wives do this. This is why it doesn't sound strange to ask someone, *How's your marriage?* But, think about how awkward it sounds to ask, *How's your co-parenting relationship?* This is because of our culture. We assume separated parents have conflict and that it isn't a good relationship. We assume it isn't worth focusing on in the same ways we do other relationships. While people spend much energy fretting about what they can do to improve romantic relationships, the co-parenting relationship is ignored because people put the blame on the other parent, someone they assume is out of their control of influence. But, really? Is it not important? Aren't our children worth as much as our pursuit of intimacy in marriage relationships?

When couples go to therapy, they often have clarity about their issues and the ability to deal with them. But, sometimes they are engaging with the issues in a manner which doesn't lead to a satisfying resolution. Going to therapy is less about having the therapist give them the answer and more about guiding the process through which they seek the solution. Many times this is a wise choice and a good use of a therapist. But, you actually don't need a therapist for this. Even without a therapist, I strongly recommend that you begin, and continue, the *process conversation*.

The process conversation is not about issues. Through your interactions with your other parent, you are generally focused on issues and this is normal. You certainly need to share information and negotiate toward specific agreements. However, you are always involved in a negotiation *about* the negotiation. On some level, each interaction is a way of negotiating *how* you interact. This is why I call it the process conversation. It is focused on the process, rather than the issues. Therapists make this explicit, which is often why therapy is helpful for clients. There can be great benefit from focusing on *how* you engage, regardless of the content. And, this focus on process can slow down the interaction in order to help you have more of a sense of control in steering the process in a positive direction.

When two people engage in ongoing conflict, they often develop habitual patterns. When conflicts occur, these patterns happen seemingly automatically. You might recognize this in your interactions with your other parent. The fight, while unpleasant and leading to unsatisfying outcomes, is very familiar. It often unfolds in a very similar way, regardless of the issue. You two are involved in what I would call a type of game. There is a pattern to the interaction. It tends to go a particular way. And, in the middle, you may not have a sense of being in control. You may think that it is happening along some rules and you can't interrupt or change it. This is similar to playing an actual game. If we start a game of Monopoly, it will unfold with some particular content. But, it will follow the general rules of Monopoly. It won't start to look like Chess or Sorry or Hungry, Hungry, Hippos. We might wish it had different features, but it will flow along like most Monopoly games do until it reaches a Monopoly-specific resolution, fun or not. This is similar to your conflicts with your other parent. And, it's another reason therapists are often helpful. We slow down, and even interrupt, the game. When you slow down the game, people renegotiate the process. People feel more in control of the process and see that they are making choices in the middle of it, that it is not happening outside them. Let me explain further.

I was involved in mediating an intense conflict between two parents. Like many parents, each had strong animosity toward the other and expressed this through harsh language. When speaking to the mother, the father consistently called her, *You Shithead!* When speaking to the father, the mother consistently called him, *You Asshole!* I had the sense that they had been using these terms with each other for a long time. At the beginning of the negotiation, I saw this language as unhelpful. So, I focused on the process and requested that they stop using these terms and switch to using the other parent's first name. They rolled their eyes at me, but complied.

As soon as they did this, the level of conflict came down several notches. This simple change had a profound effect on their ability to focus successfully on the issues at hand.

Regardless of the content, process is important. Of course, the lesson here can be: Look for features of your process that are not serving you well, and shift them so they are not getting in the way. The example of the two parents speaking harshly to each other is, perhaps, too strong compared to your situation. But, I am guessing you can find similar features of your dynamic with your other parent that, regardless of the content, cause your process to get derailed. Try to become interested in solving this part of the game. Unlike Monopoly, you *can* change the rules as you go along. And, you should. You should be constantly looking for and modifying your process so that you move toward a stable, workable co-parenting relationship. I believe this is your responsibility, even if it seems that the other parent is not responding with the same care. Sometimes the ball *is* on your side of the net and you can decide whether, and how, to knock it back across.

Another application of this focus on process is having an actual conversation that puts your process out on the table. If you do so, you and your other parent can work with it, directly. It is beneficial to do this for several reasons.

You should use your own language, but I suggest delivering (in person or via e-mail) the following message: *Look, I know that we have had a lot of conflict about parenting. We don't always come to agreements. Sometimes we fight when it probably isn't helpful. I know you have some issues with me and I have some with you about how we try to do this. I agree to try to work to improve how we relate to each other for the sake of our children. This is complicated and we'll probably screw up sometimes. But, I think we really need to do what we can to improve our co-parenting.* A message like this puts the process out as something to work with, regardless of the content that may be relevant for you now, or in the future. It opens up a dialog, not about a particular issue, but about how you try to deal with issues. It isn't a one-time message or conversation, but an ongoing re-evaluation of how you are doing as two separated parents trying to craft a more workable relationship. It doesn't solve any issues. But, I believe having this process conversation is important for you to make *how* you co-parent a legitimate focus in addition to the *what* of your co-parenting. It lets the other parent know that you take co-parenting seriously and are working from your end to improve the relationship. And, it lets the other parent know that you are holding them accountable for their end of the dynamic. It also conveys understanding that what you are attempting to accomplish is complicated. It acknowledges that complications are normal and expected, not necessarily proof of failure.

# 7 DOING CONFLICT WELL

When we are engaged in conflict, we are sometimes focused on goals and sometimes the relationship. We may be focused on both the goal and the relationship. Or, we may be trying to avoid the conflict, altogether. If we look at how we tend to react to and navigate conflicts, we notice that each of us has an individual style. We tend to react to various conflicts in particular ways. If you are interested in getting better at achieving more desirable outcomes (winning goals and preserving the relationship), learn about your style. When you understand your style, you can see how that style influences both the process and outcome of a particular conflict. Sometimes our style fits well with a particular situation. Sometimes it doesn't. It is also helpful to understand the style of your other parent. Knowing their preferred style helps you engage with them in ways that best supports mutually satisfying outcomes.

There are several conflict style approaches. The one I use in my practice is the Kraybill Conflict Style Inventory. This inventory indicates a score for *calm* and *storm* style preferences. Each of us has a preferred style for dealing with low-level conflicts. Many of us have a secondary style that we adopt if our first-line style doesn't seem to be working or if it is a moderate- or high-level conflict. No style is the best for all situations. When we learn about the styles we tend to use less often, we can develop them as options to employ when a situation seems to call for it. Having a sense of more choice and skill will lead to better outcomes and less stress. The five styles as defined in the Kraybill inventory are:

**Directing**: If this is your preferred style, you will typically be focused on your own agenda or goal. There is low, or no, focus on the relationship. This is a win/lose style. It is more useful in urgent and important situations. If the house is on fire, I don't care if you like the way I throw you out the window, the goal is to save your life. If you use this style in most situations, including those that are less urgent or important, others tend to either become dependent, or annoyed that their concerns aren't respected. If your other parent uses this style, she or he will be task and goal oriented. You will need to be assertive if you need to slow down the process when she or he is impatient and pushing for a resolution. You will need to push for a process that preserves the relationship, even if it seems that she or he is ignoring it in focusing on the goal.

**Cooperating**: If cooperating is your preferred style, you will focus on the issues *and* the relationship. You can tolerate different views and consider other's perspectives. You can take time to allow all parties to give substantive input toward a mutually satisfying solution. This is oriented toward a win/win solution. This style is useful in situations that are complex and full of important issues and where the ongoing relationship is of lasting importance. Being successful co-parents will rely on you two adopting a cooperative process most of the time since you face many, complex issues and need to deal with each other effectively for years to come. Cooperating takes communication and conflict skills and may take more time than other styles. When people attempt cooperation and fail, it may reduce hope about the future relationship. However, the answer is to increase communication and negotiation skills as described in this book. Persevere as the reward is essential for your children.

If your other parent prefers cooperating, celebrate! This is a good situation. It may not seem like it if you have a strong preference for directing, avoiding, or harmonizing. But, for issues of moderate to high importance, cooperating is the best style. Your cooperating other parent may want to negotiate in detail about issues of low importance, too. If that's true, sort your issues and persuade him or her to be flexible about those that matter less. Endless negotiations get exhausting for everyone, regardless of preferred style. There are so many important issues on which you two must focus, dropping some of the less important ones can get you some relief.

**Compromising**: If compromising is your style, you are willing to give up some if you get some of what you want. It may be a short-term choice to approximate the more desirable style of collaboration when there either isn't time to fully collaborate, or if attempts at collaboration fail. It is a win/win/lose/lose strategy since you both get part, but not all, of what you want. It is more useful for issues of medium importance. It is also important in the short-term if preserving the relationship is essential and a decision of a complex issue needs to be settled. In the long-term, the lose/lose part of the outcome becomes more of a problem.

I see many parents settle into a pattern of compromise since the alternatives seem less desirable both in terms of losing goals and eroding the quality of the relationship. This can be beneficial in the sense that it fosters an ongoing sense of fairness. The cost is the series of losses that result from compromise. In particular negotiations, parents sometimes get highly focused on having the other parent compromise in order to have that sense of fairness, regardless of the substance of the issue. If compromise is your preferred style, this is a pitfall.

There have been many mediation sessions in which I have seen parents get mired in complicated conflict just because they want to see compromise. Mutually satisfying agreements sometimes happen through other processes, say cooperation. But, some parents aren't going to be satisfied because they wanted the other parent to give something up. Only when the other person agrees to a compromise will they stop pushing. Know that compromise can be better than totally losing. But, compromise, itself, should not remain the only goal.

If your other parent prefers compromise, this is better than other styles less focused on preserving the relationship. However, in situations where you believe compromise gives up something of high importance (such as an issue related to values), you need to assert yourself to promote a cooperative solution. Sometimes compromisers are motivated to get the conflict settled. You may need to pay attention to not drawing out a long, intense process if you persuade them to engage in cooperation. And, remember that a compromiser will be focused on wanting to have a sense of fairness. Help them see how cooperation supports a fair, mutually satisfying solution.

**Avoiding**: If avoiding is your style, you avoid engaging directly with conflict. This doesn't solve the conflict. It delays, or prevents, a resolution. This is most useful if the issue is of low importance. Used selectively, this style is a useful antidote to the issue of our brains being wired to overemphasize importance and urgency. This was described in an earlier chapter. We are wired to think the house is on fire in many situations when it actually isn't. One parent told me his relationship with his ex vastly improved when he had this insight: He said co-parenting was like being up to bat at a baseball game. Many times, you just stand there and let the ball sail right on by. You don't swing.

Avoiding sometimes develops as a response to the other parent having a directing style. Avoidance is a strategy for maintaining power in the dynamic. However, an Avoiding-Directing dynamic does not effectively deal with the issues and results in ongoing, high frustration. The directing parent is focused on tasks and resolutions and the avoiding parent is seen as running interference. Avoiders, like long-term compromisers, tend to have building resentment. This is because avoidance results in a lose/lose situation. Losses add up. They are not satisfying on either end.

Avoidance is often a style that parents use with each other, even if that isn't their normally preferred style in other contexts. This happens because parents sometimes communicate their displeasure with each other by refusing to cooperate. They avoid contact and meaningful dialog about issues because they are angry with each other. While non-cooperation might get that angry message across, it is not effective co-parenting. If you are angry and you think it is wise to communicate your feelings to your other parent, do it in some way other than simply refusing to cooperate with him or her. Your children need both of you actively involved in co-parenting.

I promote some avoidance, but only in the following way. Each of you needs to be constantly assessing your issues for importance and urgency. I believe important, but not urgent, issues can be sometimes put off until later. This can be useful if you need more time to calm down, deal with it at a better time, or gather important data related to the issue. So, avoidance, in the short-term, can be useful. Also, I believe that many issues are of low importance and should be avoided altogether. Pick your battles. Avoid some of them. In every case of separated parenting, there are a host of issues which will remain unresolved. Your goal is not to work out every possible issue between you. Rather, your goal is to cooperate around the important issues. Sort out the highly important ones and don't worry as much about those of low importance. It's simply not worth the conflict that will happen if you attempt to come to high agreement about everything your big brain can put on the list.

**Harmonizing**: If harmonizing is your style, you work to keep people happy. You will tend to avoid pursuing your own agenda or goals and support the agenda or goals of the other person. You will have a low tolerance of both directors and cooperators because they are too task-oriented. You prefer pleasant social interactions to business-like discussions. When someone is attempting to be cooperative, you may see this as their being directive.

Harmonizing, like avoiding, is not an effective long-term style for functional co-parenting. Your attempt to keep the other parent happy will be of limited success. And, your lack of focus on your goals reduces your needed input into the co-parenting process. It will lead to resentment toward your other parent because you are on the losing end of negotiations. Some of the time, especially around issues of low importance, harmonizing will be supportive of a good, working co-parenting relationship. Again, this choice of conflict style is best applied with careful insight into the importance of your issues.

If your other parent is a harmonizer, it may seem appealing to you in the short-term. He or she will give in and you will win. It may seem desirable to not have to deal with negotiating over the issues. However, this is not a good long-term dynamic. Your harmonizing parent will eventually resent you since she or he is always losing. And, you actually do need your other parent to be active in negotiating shared positions, not just caving in to support your being happy with the situation.

None of these styles is the best choice in all situations. We are each well served to develop the ability to adopt each one in different situations because of their particular strengths. That doesn't mean that we don't individual have a style preference. That is true for most people. And, I believe that most people have a secondary style preference to which they shift when triggered. This is one reason I use the Kraybill inventory as it measures both calm and storm responses. You might already know this about yourself. Which style do you tend to prefer? Do you shift when you go to Code Orange? If you don't know this now, observe yourself. Go to www.riverhouseepress.com and either take the online test or buy their book, which includes the test. Consider your other parent. What is her or his style? How can you best approach her or him in order to best deal with shared co-parenting concerns?

*During Conflicts, Focus on the Goal AND the Future Relationship*

Keep these two aspects of conflict in mind. One is the *goal* (easy) and the other is the *relationship* (not so easy). Even in situations where the relationship doesn't seem to matter (because you are dealing with someone you don't expect to have to encounter again), it actually will matter *during* the negotiation so that the process can continue in hopes of reaching a mutually satisfying agreement. For example, if you took a long road trip, had a mechanical problem with your car, and found yourself haggling over a seemingly over-priced repair estimate, you would need to negotiate with the relationship in mind. Sure, you might not expect to drive that way again and have to deal with the people at that particular garage. But, if you treat the other party so badly during the negotiation that they become unwilling to negotiate to your advantage, then you will get a less optimal outcome.

Of course, when dealing with the other parent, you are dealing with someone with whom you share a child (or children). Depending on the age of your youngest shared child, you may have to deal with each other for many years. And, even when children are adults, they want their parents to be able to get along at their wedding or, even farther into future, at *their* children's graduation.

As separated parents, you are operating at a disadvantage. High stress tends to shut down the part of your brain most devoted to relating with empathy toward others, thinking positively, and thinking out into the future. The legal system sets you up to be adversaries and to focus on explicit issues, not your relationship (for example, defining the parenting time schedule). Attorneys and mediators also focus on legal goals. And, there may be seemingly urgent and important goals that reasonably draw your attention. This all adds up to a tendency to be focused on goals to the exclusion of the relationship. Past, unresolved conflicts might also get in the way of your having much hope for a positive relationship. You may not trust the other parent to be a collaborative co-parent. So, it is not unusual if you see a focus on the relationship as fruitless while pursuing goals as having immediate value.

It is important to focus on your goals *and* your relationship. In practical terms, what does this mean? One way to maintain this dual focus is to know that your brain is wired to help you lose sight of the quality of the future co-parenting relationship when you are triggered and focused on the goal right in front of you. Being conscious of this pitfall can help you notice it and correct for it by remembering to think about how your current interactions with the other parent may influence your ability to collaborate in the future. Sometimes losing a battle in the short-term is better for a long-term outcome.

The process of legal divorce is generally focused on goals to the exclusion of the co-parenting relationship. You will have to keep your frontal lobe online to promote a better co-parenting relationship. Don't get caught up in thinking that the legal view is the only view (I will discuss this in chapter eleven in greater detail).

Another benefit of remembering to focus on the relationship is that some co-parenting strategies have more to do with the relationship than solving issues. For example, I'll describe in the next chapter the value of thanking your other parent for specific behaviors. This is not necessarily instrumental in dealing with a particular issue. But, it is of great value in crafting a positive relationship. If you are exclusively focused on goals, you will not attend to the relationship and it will suffer, not grow.

This lack of focus on the relationship is another big factor of why so many parents are not more civil when communicating with each other. It's not only that parents don't feel positively toward each other (though that matters). It's because their concern about the relationship has gone out the window. Compare it to a situation when you might be dealing with a boss whom you don't really like very much. In an interaction with this boss, you might not be as friendly as you are with your actual good friends. But, you will remain civil. This is because you preserve a focus on the relationship (you want to keep your job). If the concern about the relationship goes away, you might tell your boss where to stick his issue and walk out the door. If you did so, maybe you are lucky and can replace this job with another where you have a boss you like better. But, in your co-parenting relationship, you can't quit. You have to deal with each other for years to come. So, maintain your focus on the quality of the relationship even while you are focused on goals. To disregard this is to prolong nasty, unsatisfying conflict. And, do it even if the other parent doesn't seem to be doing so from their end.

I highly recommend that you read *Getting Together: Building Relationships as We Negotiate* by Roger Fisher and Scott Brown. While this book is aimed at people involved in formal mediation, it has many useful strategies helpful to separated parents. For example, I like Fisher and Brown's explanation of the failure of the Golden Rule in negotiations. You know the Golden Rule: *Treat others as you would have them treat you.* In conflicts, this gets turned around and results in a tit-for-tat dynamic. It morphs into: *I will treat you as I think you are treating me.* This is very, very unhelpful. It results in unending conflict which damages the negotiating relationship. You should, rather, preserve a rule of: *I will treat you in a manner which I think will enhance our negotiating relationship, even if I perceive you to not be acting in the same way.* There are many helpful ideas in their book. And, I suggest you also read *Getting to Yes: Negotiating Agreement without Giving In* by Roger

Fisher, William L. Ury, and Bruce Patton, and *Getting Past No* by William Ury. Both of those books have additional resources applicable to separated parenting. They also may help you in other areas of your life in which you have to negotiate with other people. In the next section, I will explain another method for enhancing your co-parenting relationship, which I call: *the process conversation*.

*Focus on The Issue, Not the Person*

Avoid attacking people, even when they deserve it. It is easy to lose sight of the issue and be mostly focused on the person with whom you are having conflict. This is another way that our brains are wired to identify and deal with sources of danger. But, it will not serve you well when dealing with your other parent. Basically, I see parents dealing with each other often by complaining and telling each other, *You suck*!

This is not news to you. You already know that it doesn't feel good to be personally attacked. And, it makes you less, not more, cooperative. But, even though all of us know this, we don't act as though it's true. You will be well-served to remember this and avoid attacking your other parent.

My advice to parents is to end conversations if they descend into personal attacks. It is useless to continue such an interaction. I believe this to be an essential agreement parents must make with each other: to avoid calling each other names or being otherwise verbally abusive. When your other parent delivers what seems like a personal attack in a more mild form, you can attempt to steer the conversation back to the issue. If she or he refuses, then end the interaction. It is damaging for your children to witness such an interaction. And, even in the absence of your children, attacking each other serves no positive purpose.

Know that fairness doesn't mean that it is OK to deliver a personal attack on the other person when they do it to you. If you wait until your other parent seems to have stopped doing this, you will continue in a damaging way. I believe each parent has an individual responsibility to avoid personal attacks, *even if the other parent doesn't seem to be doing the right thing.* Remember that I have explained that you are likely to continue to see negativity even when your other parent is making a good effort to avoid it. So, responding with negativity in-kind only slows your ability to steer your co-parenting relationship in a positive direction. And, in the end, I don't care if your other parent only *seems* to not be doing it, or is *really* not doing it. You must choose to avoid delivering personal attacks from your end, anyway.

# 8 DEALING WITH THE LEGAL SYSTEM

Many separated parents find themselves on the losing end of the legal system. It often doesn't provide satisfying solutions and may cost dearly in dollars and increased complications. Many parents swirl through the legal process for months or years, damaging their ability to co-parent. Approximately one-third of parents are still litigating their divorces five years after separation. At six years one-quarter are still at it. This points to ongoing hostility and inability—or unwillingness—to solve their conflicts outside of court. In this chapter I will explain common issues related to involvement with the legal system as separated parents. It is not intended to serve as legal advice relevant to your particular case or as a prediction for what outcomes you might experience in the courts. But, please use legal advice and the legal system wisely for the sake of your children.

You may find it useful to understand how the legal system relates to separated co-parenting. I will explain common issues that exist when parents take their disputes to the legal arena. While I'll discuss this more richly below, my short advice is this: Avoid the legal system when you can. And, use it for what it can do. Seek elsewhere for the things it won't likely provide. First, a history lesson that explains a common dynamic in legal cases involving battling, separated parents.

## How Did We Get into This Mess?

The most common dynamic I see in cases which involve parents battling in the courts is where the mother works to get the court to see that the father is either controlling or uninvolved and the father works to get the courts to see that the mother is crazy. This is usually a tactic to try to win a greater amount of parenting time than the other parent. Here's one factor that contributes to that dynamic: *history*.

During a large portion of our country's history (up until the early 1900s), custody disputes over children were simple—at least from a legal standpoint. In the eyes of the courts, children were no different than tangible property. And, through most of that era, women were not allowed to own property acquired during a legal marriage. So, this made custody disputes pretty cut and dried.

Then along came weirdos like Sigmund Freud who complicated all of that with psychological theories such as: *children are not merely property and not merely younger and smaller versions of adults…they are fragile people because the are going through early stages of life when they will need essential nurturance from caregivers.* Freud thought that good development could only happen if the child was properly attached to her caregivers during these early years. Lack of attachment could lead to one becoming neurotic as an adult. These ideas are still very popular in our society.

So, with good intentions, the courts applied these theories and no longer defaulted to giving fathers custody of children as property. They flipped and by default gave custody to mothers because direct parenting of young children was generally provided by mothers. (Now, I'm pleased to report that fathers are becoming increasingly involved with young children and the research shows that this is a very good thing, but this is a somewhat recent trend—go ask your father how many diapers he changed when you and your siblings were young.) Because attachment was seen as so crucial to early development, judges peered out across the bench and attempted to discern to which parent the child was most attached. It was often the mother. So, the trend shifted with mothers tending to win disputed custody. But, here's the twist…

This wasn't about a theoretical shift simply away from fathers in favor of mothers (though many people do hold that bias). It was a shift into seeing the importance of attachment for young children. It was our culture (Dads tending to work outside the home and moms tending to stay at home with young children) that resulted in the skewed perceptions of the courts. That mom-centered bias wouldn't have happened in the same way if we had lived in a society where moms and dads equally shared in diaper changing (and other aspects of direct parenting of younger children).

However we got here, this focus on attachment meant that the parent who could prove to the court that they had the most strongly attached relationship with the child would win custody. Moms have generally benefited from this view. But, when custody or parenting time is in dispute in the courts, moms are usually wanting to prove to the court that the children aren't very attached to dad, or that he is so controlling that he prevents them from being attached to him and also controls their ability to be attached to her. Dads usually fight back with the strategy: *Yes, the child is more attached to mom, but she's batshit crazy and an unfit parent!*

I'm hoping this doesn't describe your case. But, it might. And, if this is your dynamic, you will probably both be quite sincere in your view that the other parent is really too absent, controlling, unstable, or crazy to have a reasonable relationship with your children. I'm not saying all complaints about parents are trivial and shouldn't ever be brought up in court. But, I am saying that the way the courts shape these battles has predictable consequences for parents. And, rather than solving disputes, it is often quite damaging to the co-parenting relationship.

If you come to view the other parent in these negative modes (promoted by the courts), you will react to her/him as such. It goes against everything I've promoted so far in this book. The courts make it more, not less, likely that you will view the other parent as evil, stupid, and crazy. It will seem like it is to your legal advantage to do so. And, playing out that strategy is going to be felt like one of the worst attacks a person can experience. You will also be the target of the other parent and it will feel awful. I have seen very functional people, even with a good history of collaborative parenting, become bitter enemies because of the harsh attacks they directed toward each other in the court process. Parents usually see the other parent as lying. And, not merely lying (however bad one might think it is to be dishonest), but lying with the intent to make the other parent look like a bad parent. The goal is often to cause the other parent to lose custody or parenting time. Few things in life are more triggering than the threat of separation from your child. This is how court can be so very damaging. Now we are shifting into a new era. After most of a century of mostly looking at attachment, the legal system has offered a new term: *Best Interests of the Child*. I'll say more about this below, but first I'll discuss how inappropriate it is to ask a child to decide custody. This is another damaging strategy that many parents use to win in the courts.

*When Can Our Child Decide Custody?*

There is an persistent urban myth in our society that says that children magically wake up on their twelfth or fourteenth birthdays having been transformed into competent custody evaluators. Not true! Not true! Let me say it, again…***NOT TRUE!!!***

I wish that were all I needed to say on the subject. But, experience has shown me that people who believe it won't take that simple answer. Why? Because the people who believe this myth are hearing words come out of their child's mouth consistent with their own position on custody or parenting time. Usually they celebrate it with expectant satisfaction because they think they're about to get over on their ex as soon as their child has their next birthday. Parents will offer all sorts of logic to pull in the child because they think they'll get what they want if the child gets a voice. It is wrong for multiple reasons. Let me give you a case that helps make this point, but with child younger than the typical twelve-year old...

I got a referral from two attorneys who were working with a set of parents who were divorcing and shared a seven-year old daughter. The parents were relatively amicable and not in dispute of very much, though each was about to petition the court for primary physical custody. They had mutually agreed to share joint legal custody (shared decision making) but each parent wanted to have the child on overnights the majority of the time. Their attorneys suggested they come speak to me before filing the petitions. A mediated solution would likely help them avoid a nasty court battle since they were in agreement about pretty much every other aspect of their case. They came to see me and this is how it went...

First appointment: Father arrives. I ask, "So, why are you thinking of filing a petition for primary physical custody?" He replies, "Well, Jon, our daughter has a great relationship with her mom and I support that very much. But, most times when she's at my house she tells me the same thing: 'Dad, swear to me you won't tell mom this because I love her and don't want to hurt her feelings, but after you two get divorced, make sure I'm at your house most of the time.'" You may be guessing where this is going, and no I am not making this up...these are the words of the clients.

Two days later: Mother arrives. I ask, "So, why are you thinking of filing a petition for primary physical custody?" She replies, "Well, Jon, our daughter has a great relationship with her dad and I support that very much. But, most times when she's at my house she tells me the same thing: 'Mom, swear to me you won't tell dad this because I love him and don't want to hurt his feelings, but after you two get divorced, make sure I'm at your house most of the time.'"

So, let's get this straight. Each of these parents was about to march into court and open up a hostile battle to win primary physical custody and justify that move based solely on the words coming out of their seven-year old's mouth. They were going to do this legal battle, even at the risk of severely, maybe permanently, damaging an otherwise very workable post-separation co-parenting relationship. I call this: *Handing your brain over to a seven-year old!*

Imagine this: You have an important court hearing coming up. And, you go to your attorney's office on the morning of the hearing because you and she had scheduled a strategy session. As you walk into her office, she is running out the door. You say, "Hey, we have a hearing today and need to meet. Where are you going?" She replies, "Don't worry. There's a seven-year old sitting in my office. Talk to him. He'll give you great advice."

You would, hopefully, fire that attorney and try to postpone the hearing. You wouldn't casually trust your life in the hands of a seven-year old. But, parents do this all the time during and after separation. I have seen this over and over. It's a bad idea, but for even more reasons than what I've explained so far.

**Reason One to not ask a child to make a consequential legal decision for embattled adults**: *They are incompetent, lacking life experience and playing juvenile developmental games.* Younger kids, like seven-year olds, play the game of: *I'm old enough to know that my actions sometimes hurt others' feelings, so I'll try to not do that to Mommy or Daddy.* Older kids are playing games like the twelve-year old common game of *play both ends against the middle*.

**Reason Two**: To the extent that children think they are influencing the decisions around the divorce, they will soon feel responsible. It's not that it *might* happen. It *will* happen. Here's why I think this…

A typical scenario: A mother and father are in dispute of primary physical custody (and maybe many other things). Their son is asked to state a preference which he gladly does (because he's 13 and one parent has a nicer house which is also closer to the places he likes to hang out with his friends). The parents get an order from the court which supports the son's (and one of the parent's) position. However, this is no Shangri-La. After the nasty court battle, the parents are even more hostile and less cooperative with each other. They fight in front of the son more often and with greater hostility. It's obvious to the son that they are fighting about the custody outcome. He will feel responsible for it. It was a lose/lose scenario for him as soon as his parents asked him to state his preference.

But this belief doesn't die easily. Let me tell you what happens most of the time when I get to this point in explaining this issue to a parent who wants to bring a child into the court proceedings.

The next thing I usually hear is this: *"I'm really not doing this for me, I'm doing it because it's best for the child."*

**Reason Three**: Even if they weren't incompetent (which they are, even if they seem to be agreeing with you in this moment), their position in the situation puts them at a disadvantage in making such a decision. Look at it this way: If you hired a custody evaluator to come interview you and your other parent in order to make recommendations to the court, you would share a lot of sensitive information with the evaluator. We evaluators need to ask a lot of detailed questions about your situation in order to offer the best possible recommendations. This is why we often will meet with parents without the children present. We will need to ask questions and discuss some material that the children should not be exposed to, however relevant it is to the situation. So, if you and the other parent are doing the responsible job that you should be doing and keeping from your children thing they don't need to hear (now, and perhaps ever!) about the divorce, then your children are in no position to offer a competent recommendation about custody or parenting time. In no way should you see this as an invitation to share this type of information with your children. Quite the opposite. I want you to share as little as possible with your children. Parents usually are way, way too open with their children about details of the separation. It's not really achievable, but try to steer toward having oblivious children. Their short-term stress related to not getting all their questions answered will by far be outweighed by the benefit of their being spared your complications and drama. Again, I never have met an adult whose parents got divorced when she/he was a child who told me, *I really wish my parents would have been more open with me about the details of their divorce and shared more of their sadness, confusion, and anger with* *me. That would have made my life so much better.* I NEVER hear that. It's always the opposite.

**Reason Four**: It is normal for children to have a different relationship with each parent. I assume you would report this was true for you: that you have a different relationship with each of your parents and early caregivers. It is normal and doesn't mean that something dysfunctional needs to be fixed.

At the point of separation, children will often have a different relationship with each parent and this may be a difference in level and quality of attachment. Asking the child to express an interest will be asking the child to indicate the parent to whom they are more attached or with whom that attachment is experienced as less complicated. Again, this is not sufficient data on which to base a custody or parenting time decision. It is relevant. This type of information can help parents craft a better custody and parenting time agreement. But, it is insufficient. And, it should be explored by the adults in the situation, not handed over to the child to find the answer.

One other bit of advice I will offer around litigation is: Don't ever show your children your court papers! Never! Parents who do this usually justify it by telling me: *I have an open, honest relationship with my child. I never lie to him/her.* This is not a valid excuse. Every instance of parents showing court papers to children has been one version or another of: *I'm right. Your other parents is wrong. And, here's the paper to prove it! The judge, the most powerful person in the land, agrees with me!* This is an extremely damaging thing to communicate to your child. Don't do it! Your child should, maybe, read your court papers when, as an adult (and with no help from you whatsoever) they figure out that divorce proceedings are public record. Maybe if they are older and doing a family tree and come across the information it is OK. But, even then, it will likely be troubling for them to read. Don't show them your papers!

There are instances when court decisions must be carefully discussed with children. If, for example, a judge orders a change in parenting time, this must be communicated in a supportive and compassionate way to children. It must be communicated in a way that does not denigrate the other parent. If you are not up to doing that in a good way for your child, see a therapist for support in having that conversation.

*Parental Alienation Syndrome*

For many years Parental Alienation Syndrome (PAS) was promoted by Richard Gardner. In short, PAS was alleged to be a syndrome wherein children were brainwashed by one parent into believing and making false allegations of (sexual and physical) abuse against the other parent. Many of Gardner's assertions on which he built his theory run counter to empirical research and widely supported theory. Gardner claimed to be able to definitively differentiate between true and false allegations of abuse, though his method was widely rejected as invalid in the mental health community. Gardner also offered very severe recommendations in cases in which he believed PAS existed, such as removing the child from the home of the parent to whom she is aligned and place her in primary custody of the parent she alleged abused her as well as subjecting the child to reverse brain-washing to convince her she wasn't abused. PAS has been popular in the father's rights movement since allegations of abuse are more often against mothers.

PAS is another unfortunate aspect of our culture of adversarial divorce and conflict-driven post-separation parenting. I do not believe PAS to be a valid mental health construct and I think that the consequences of applying the concept of PAS is misguided and damaging to healthy co-parenting.

Children are often alienated from one parent during and after separation. This estrangement can occur for many reasons. Sometimes, the relationship between the child and the parent was already complicated and worsened post-separation. Divorce researcher Judith Wallerstein, in her books *Surviving the Break-up – How Children and Parents Cope with Divorce* and *The Unexpected Legacy of*

*Divorce*, explains that alignment is typical after divorce, is usually against the parent who the child thinks initiated the divorce, and usually resolves with no intervention within one to two years.

The parent to whom the child is closer should not be interfering with that process. But, PAS offers a troubling solution: to diagnose with a mental health disorder the parent to whom the child is closer. This is typically the mother and I believe promoted as part of the dynamic I described at the beginning of the chapter in which the father attempts to gain power in the situation by convincing the courts that the mother is crazy.

Please do understand I am not trying to trivialize alienation of a child from their parent. Speaking and behaving badly toward your other parent in ways that interferes with your child's relationship with them is wrong and it is your responsibility to clean this up now. If you are on the receiving end of this behavior and your child is consequently alienated from you, I do believe that this is a reasonable issue to address. But, however objectionable and damaging such behavior, I do not agree that it rises to the level of mental health dysfunction in the same way we consider someone meeting the criteria for Panic Disorder or a Depressive Disorder. There is consensus around this, too. Mental health professionals do not acknowledge Gardner's construct, though there is a vocal minority of people pushing for this recognition.

I sincerely hope you never have to defend yourself against PAS in the courts. However, Gardner did gain a significant following in the father's rights movement as well as many attorneys and judges. Now that he is dead, perhaps his harmful ideas and recommendations will fade away. If you find yourself dealing with allegations of PAS, I suggest you also read Carol Bruch's article *Parental Alienation Syndrome and Parental Alienation: Getting It Wrong in Child Custody Cases* published in Family Law Quarterly (Fall, 2001, Volume 35, Edition 3).

*Father's Rights*

For the past few decades, there have been a variety of people and groups promoting father's rights in the context of post-divorce co-parenting. Diverse opinions and goals exist within this movement. But, in general, the concerns focus on issues within society and the legal system which many people believe result in unfair biases against fathers after divorce. Many of the goals of the father's rights movement are reasonable. For example, plenty of research shows that children tend to have better social, physical, academic, mental health, and developmental outcomes when both parents are involved in their lives. If the father's rights movement succeeds in making it possible for more children to have both parents meaningfully involved in their lives, then that is a good thing. However, there is not good research support for some of the assertions of the movement. So far, research has not clearly supported the idea that a fifty-fifty split of parenting time is significantly better than an uneven parenting time schedule. However desirable an even split of parenting time is from the parents' points of view, it has yet to be shown to be essential or correlated with any particular developmental outcome. To be clear, when it can work logistically and in the context of a collaborative co-parenting relationship, I am not opposed to even splits of parenting time. It is a fair way to divide parenting tasks. And, it certainly does afford children ample access to both parents.

*So, Should We Get A Custody Evaluation?*

Sometimes, parents in dispute of custody or parenting time seek a professional custody evaluation. It is important to understand what such an evaluation is and isn't. It is also helpful to think about the risks involved and limitations. Unfortunately, a custody evaluation isn't the magic bullet to solve ongoing difficulties between separated parents.

A custody evaluation is a report typically prepared by a professional who has experience in divorce cases and who often will offer recommendations around custody, parenting time, and related issues. Usually, a custody evaluator is a psychologist, social worker, or psychotherapist with qualifications and credentials to assess psychosocial issues in individuals and families. Currently, there is no licensure or credentialing at the state level for custody evaluators. The safeguards for clients reside in the professional organizations in which the evaluator may retain membership and in the courts which hold such evaluations to a minimal level of acceptable quality. That is, the evaluator is expected to not be practicing outside her or his area of training and credentialing.

If you participate in a custody evaluation, you are likely to be assessed individually in terms of your mental health status. Your children will likely be similarly assessed, though parents are often assessed through a different evaluative lens. If a psychologist is performing the evaluation or participating as a consultant, parents may be asked to complete a standardized mental health assessment tool called the Minnesota Multiphasic Personality Inventory (MMPI) in addition to subjective mental health interviewing by the evaluator. The MMPI returns a set of scores which are interpreted by a competent clinician, often a psychologist. The interpretation sometimes has useful information that is relevant to the parents' mental health status or their ability to parent as separated parents.

Whatever the type of evaluation that is applied to determine the parents' mental health status, it is understood that parents tend to be viewed, even by experienced clinicians, as more dysfunctional at the time of separation—and during ongoing, high-conflicts—than they might at other times of their lives or in other situations. This interferes with the validity of the assessment. Ideally, a useful evaluation will have relevance on current issues (for example a dispute over parenting time) and also support, not interfere with, ongoing, workable co-parenting. However, it is challenging to perform an objective evaluation that functions this way.

Parents may have issues which are not clear to the evaluator through the evaluation process. These, then, will not be directly addressed in the evaluation or recommendations. Or, parents may appear dysfunctional in the process of the evaluation in a way that does not need to be addressed. The evaluator, the courts, and the parents are interested in keeping the case on track. And, it is unfortunate when a custody evaluation contributes to an adversarial relationship. Many times, though, this is the case.

Custody evaluations are most helpful when the courts need an expert to clarify issues that impact the disputes being addressed in hearings. If an evaluation helps clarify, for instance, that a child has a problematic relationship with one of the parents, then that issue might be addressed directly as a result. If issues that impact wise choices around parenting time are clarified, then scheduling recommendations are sometimes helpful. For example, if the evaluation reveals that the parents have difficulty cooperating around a specific issue (getting the child to school on time, or choosing a pediatrician), then the evaluation might resolve the issue.

There are limitations to custody evaluations. If the fundamental issue between two parents is ongoing hostility and an inability to cooperate effectively, the evaluation is not likely to offer a satisfying resolution. In that case, the evaluation is typically not needed to show the pattern of hostility as it was already clear before. And, evaluation recommendations, like court orders, are of limited usefulness in increasing co-parental cooperation. However desirable it is for all involved for the parents to get along and co-parent effectively, the evaluator can't command them to do so. Neither can the courts.

Evaluations can also be complicating if they result in future battles in the courts. When recommendations are written into court orders, they sometimes become additional issues around which parents fight. While I am not discouraging all parents to avoid seeking a competent custody evaluation if it seems useful, I do think parents should consider how specific they want the court to be in writing orders. Too many specific orders from the court invite additional future petitions due to non-compliance.

Too often, parents seek a change in custody to resolve an issue that ought to be pursued in another manner. In my experience, the majority of cases in which parents are seeking a change in custody involve an issue that won't be resolved no matter what the outcome in the court. When a custody evaluation is brought into the process, it raises risks, costs money, and is unsatisfying. For example, a recent case involved a parent who was seeking a change of custody and trying to compel the other parent to submit to a custody evaluation because he thought his ex-wife was "crazy." The parent explained to me that he and his daughter had a "really bad relationship" and the mother was "ruining it" by saying bad things about him to the daughter. At the time of his petition, the mother had primary physical custody and the father was exercising state guidelines parenting time per the normal schedule—every other weekend and one mid-week, four-hour time.

The father was petitioning the court to reverse the parenting time schedule so he would have the majority of parenting time and the mother would have the guidelines for a non-custodial parent. From where I was sitting, I didn't see how such a change would help the father with the issue of the problematic relationship with his daughter. If it were true that the mother was the main factor, she would still have ample opportunity to say bad things about him to the daughter with his proposed change in custody. And, perhaps, he was not objective in his reasoning for the problems in his relationship with his daughter. Maybe his having more time would actually exacerbate some issue between him and the daughter, rather than enhance it.

He was promoting a nasty court battle and inviting a custody evaluation that was likely to only cost them a lot of money and not help with the fundamental issue. Another recent case involved two parents who often fought over where the child would go to school and which pediatrician she would see. While an award of sole legal custody to one parent might resolve the technical issue of which parent could ultimately make such decisions, it was clear to me that these parents had a general inability to cooperate. I did not see how any sort of change in custody would help that.

The legal bar for a change of custody is fairly high. What this means is that parents who are seeking a modification of a prior custody order must deliver a very strong and compelling case to the court. This will typically be a hostile attack on the other parent. These types of court processes are very damaging to the co-parental relationship. In many cases they permanently damage the relationship. It never recovers. If you are considering a petition to modify custody, you must think very carefully about whether such a change really will directly address the issue which is causing problems. You must also expect that any custody battle will be an extremely complicating experience for you and the other parent to weather. In my experience, less than one-quarter of such actions were even reasonable to consider. Sit down and contemplate the outcome. If you get exactly what you want from the court, is it possible you'll still be dealing with exactly the same issue? Ask yourself this question and ponder it carefully before you launch into a legal process that will come with financial and emotional costs and which could severely damage the workability of your co-parenting relationship. It may be better, sometimes, to explore other strategies to solve your issues. I'll explore seeking therapy, using mediation, and what happens if other people become involved in your case.

## *Will Therapy Help Our Co-parenting Relationship?*

Some separated parents seek support from a family therapist or social worker to resolve post-separation conflicts. This is sometimes helpful but, often, isn't helpful at all. First, let me address a general issue that applies for parents seeking therapy—as well as when children are brought to therapy—during, or after, separation.

If you bring your children to therapy, be clear about your motivations with the therapist about what is happening in your case, especially as it pertains to legal actions. Therapy for children should be about offering the child support for their experience of and reactions to the separation of parents. There are times when this is helpful, though the younger the child, the less they tend to benefit from adult-style talk therapy. The therapist you contact will use their judgment about whether or not the therapy is helpful and hopefully will recommend not applying a therapeutic process if it isn't warranted. But, know two things. First, no therapist has a crystal ball to be able to know objectively what is up with the other parent merely by talking to your child. Bringing a child to therapy to dig for dirt on the other parent is an extremely bad motive. And, it happens often. I hope this is not your thinking, but bringing a child to therapy with this motive is just another way of putting the child in the middle. Also, to the extent that the child is developed enough to see this game, she or he will refuse to participate in order to avoid being caught in the middle. And, know that teens are often reluctant to engage with the therapist which adds another adult to their roster of people they have to be accountable to. Second, be very clear with the therapist if you are involved in legal proceedings involving the child. Good therapy is dependent on a safe alliance between the therapist and client. If the child worries that the therapist will be going to court to say bad things about one parent, then they will either clam up to protect the parent or, in the case that they are angry with a parent, will say overly bad or false things in order to influence that process. And, if a child is unaware of the issue of court, they will often feel betrayed or highly stressed if the therapist is brought into the court process.

So, be very careful before you allow your attorney to subpoena your therapist or their notes into the court process. In my opinion most of the time when therapists or notes are brought into the court process, it leads away from, not toward, a good outcome. Also, even in cases where the therapist seems fine going to court, what you are often getting is a set of recommendations like a custody evaluation, but with an incompetent professional. What I mean is that the child's therapist is not fully competent as a custody evaluator (to offer recommendations around custody or parenting time) because they have only a limited data stream. They have only talked with the child. Often, they have had some contact with one parent, but little to none with the other parent. This is not sufficient for a competent custody evaluation. Similarly, if you and the other parent seek therapy, do not do so with the intent to ask the therapist to go to court to say damaging things about the other parent. That is not a good use of therapy.

Another concern about accessing therapy is whether or not the therapist can competently deal with your issues as separated parents. A common complaint I hear from separated parents is that they sought post-separation therapy from someone they saw as couple before the divorce and weren't satisfied that the therapist could help them after the separation. Many therapists are helpful in addressing issues within intimate relationships but not very helpful working with separated parents. Therapy for separated parents is not properly focused on shared intimacy, but better focused on how to collaborate around all the complexities of separated co-parenting. Some therapists are more experienced and skilled at this than others. It may be helpful to inquire with a prospective therapist about their experience and approach in such situations.

The parents who seem to benefit the most from post-separation sessions with a therapist are those who need a moderator for their joint discussions. Sometimes therapists are helpful to two people involved in conflict because their presence helps tone down the stress of the conversation. Having a third party present is sometimes the most helpful aspect of therapy, even when the therapist isn't performing any particular technical skill. Also, to the extent that you and your other parent need some support in communicating effectively, the therapist is likely somewhat skilled in this area. However, if you need the therapist to address very complex post-separation issues, you may be asking them to be in a mediator role, which is different from therapy.

## *What if Others Get Involved in Our Case?*

Sometimes disputes between parents in the courts result in additional people getting involved. Even when this is for good reasons, it increases the already complicated dynamics. At first, a case involves the parents, their attorneys, and the judge. Each additional person adds additional concerns and issues. The typical people who get involved are therapists, Guardian Ad Litems or Court-appointed Special Advocates, and Parent Coordinators.

When emotional, psychological, or developmental issues are raised in court, sometimes a judge will order evaluative or therapeutic services for parents or children. As discussed above, therapy is a tricky issue if the therapist is pursuing a process that doesn't apply to the situation of separated parenting. It also can be complicated if the judge orders the parties to pursue a therapeutic goal that individual therapists don't find clinically prudent. For example, a woman involved in a divorce case arrived at my office with an order from a judge that she see a therapist to "work out her issues with men." However relevant the judge thought her "issues with men" might be in the legal sense, I had to evaluate her from a psychosocial approach to decide if it was a therapeutic goal which I could support (I didn't). The fact that a judge orders it doesn't mean it's therapeutically prudent.

Some other reasonable goals can't be solved simply because of a court order. Sometimes this takes the form of a parent alleging that the other parent has a substance abuse problem. It may be true. And, keeping substance abuse from interfering with competent and safe parenting is a worthy goal. But, an order for the parent to receive therapy to evaluate and treat their substance abuse might not be worth much if the parent is denying the alleged problem.

Sometimes judges order parents to make children available for therapy. This may be helpful if the therapist can support the child in coping with the issues of the divorce. But, each additional person involved in a case becomes a potential witness in future hearings. As described earlier in this chapter, the threat of testimony undermines good therapeutic alliances. And, the strategic attempts to use that testimony in the legal process can open the case up to complicating, unhelpful, input from those professionals. This is often a feature of disputes over custody.

Occasionally, the court will appoint a person to be an advocate of the child. These people are usually termed Guardian Ad Litems (GAL) or Court Appointed Special Advocates (CASA). These are different terms for the same role. Their role is to interact with the parents and the child in order to give input to the court about the issues facing the child. Part of the logic of such an appointment is that parents may be presenting to the court skewed information about the child's issues. The GAL is expected to be a more objective observer of the situation. They are also, sometimes, a way for the child's concerns to be considered in a court dispute without the child having the perception that they are directly involved.

A limitation to the effectiveness of the GAL is that such people are often not trained to be objective. GAL and CASA programs recruit volunteers from the community. There is no special training required, though the program may attempt to help the volunteer understand divorce cases in order to play the role more effectively. The biggest problem I have seen is that the parents often want to influence the perceptions of the volunteer and pull him or her into the adversarial process. In the best of situations, the volunteer is able to resist this and remain more objective. However, GALs do sometimes get affiliated with one side against the other. If you have such a person appointed in your case, keep them happy. Keep all appointments and know, fair or not, this person may be communicating with the court about consequential issues such as custody or parenting time.

Parent Coordinators are people sometimes appointed in divorce cases to act as managers of all services that parents and children may be receiving. They are typically professionals who have special expertise in divorce situations. They may be attorneys, or mental health professionals with special experience or education. They also can act as arbitrators of disagreements between parents. Their recommendations may be legally binding, depending on the way that they are appointed in your case. If you have such a person appointed in your case, clarify their role and what you will need to do in order to satisfy their expectations.

*Should We Use Mediation?*

Mediation helps many separated parents establish lastingly satisfying agreements while avoiding the financial and emotional costs related to litigation. Mediation is a process in which parents meet with a neutral mediator to attempt to come to agreements around various property or family matters during or after divorce or paternity litigation. Although mediation can cost several hundred dollars up front, compared to the cost of litigation, it tends to be a less-expensive approach to conflict resolution. Also, research shows that mediated agreements tend to be more lastingly satisfying to people when compared with litigated conflicts. This is not surprising since mediated agreements help people maintain a sense of control which is lost when a decision is given up to a judge. Meditation often allows participants to voice their interests in positive ways. And, mediation is less adversarial since the mediator is a neutral party, not an arbitrator or judge. Since the mediator will not render a binding decision, the process is not dominated by hostility in the same way litigation often is. It is not your job to attack the other party's position in mediation or to convince the mediator that you are right. At the end of the day, if mediation fails, the mediator is finished and will not make a binding decision.

Avoid pushing a therapist into the role of mediator. The process and goals of therapy are different from mediation. Mediation is focused on specific issues with the goal of establishing agreements. Therapy is focused on having a positive impact on the process by which you come together to attempt to come to collaborative co-parenting. Those two things are related, but different. Therapists are not necessarily good mediators and mediators are not necessarily good therapists. Both may be valuable in the same case, but better served as distinct processes.

When parents have attorneys, there is often a quasi-mediation process of back and forth communication around some disputed issues. If that process fails to produce agreement, sometimes formal mediation is advisable. When possible, talk to people who have used mediation services in your local area to get feedback on their satisfaction. Mediators have a wide range of styles and experience. Some may be more satisfying than others.

It is not necessary to have an agreement which addresses every possible issue in your situation. Mediation best serves parents focused on more important and complicated issues. However, many issues are important enough to write into an informal co-parenting plan, though not necessarily useful to include in a mediated agreement that will become a court order. Issues spelled out with a high degree of specificity in a court order help by providing structure. However, when more details are written into an order, it can make it challenging to follow or invite future petitions alleging non-compliance. See *Mom's House Dad's House* by Isolina Ricci for more discussion of developing a co-parenting plan. In short, a co-parenting plan is an informal document crafted as a result of a series of conversations or e-mail exchanges between parents that spells out agreements around whatever issues are relevant to the situation. Such agreements clarify parenting roles and responsibilities. But, you don't need mediation to come to those agreements and you might not write every one of them into a court order. For more information about mediation, see my book *The Quick Guide to Divorce Mediation*.

*Another Way to Avoid the Adversarial Legal Process*

Recently, many people have been choosing Collaborative Divorce processes to avoid costly and damaging litigation. You may have collaborative divorce practices in your local area. You can use online searches to find attorneys providing this service in your region. I suggest visiting collaborativedivorce.net for more information. In the collaborative process, parties work together to avoid adversarial litigation processes and often save money by doing so.

# 9 STRESS MANAGEMENT TECHNIQUES

I encourage you to practice stress management for three reasons. First, you need to address your overall stress level. Your stress level has been high for a long time, starting long before your actual separation. And, it will likely stay relatively high into the future. Divorce and separation entail so many stressors and, for many people, represents the most stressful period of life. This is subjectively unpleasant, not good for your health, and you will benefit psychologically (especially when dealing with your other parent) from taking steps to generally lower your ongoing, daily stress level.

It is also important to gain stress management skills in order to counteract those spikes in your stress response when interacting with your children or your other parent. Remember all the ways that I have described stress having effects on your perceptions and reactions. You will benefit from employing brief (10 seconds to five minutes long) stress management strategies in situations when you want to dial down that negative influence of stress.

And, third, you need to practice some calming techniques every day for a period of time to strengthen your brain's ability to access positive, low-stress states of mind and body. Research into the brain's ability to form and strengthen neural pathways shows that we actually change our brain structure from thinking in the same way over time. The technical term for this is: *neuroplasticity*. An example of this is a study which showed that the parts of the brain devoted to remembering where places are in space actually get bigger in the brains of taxi drivers who have to learn and remember the map of London. Other studies have shown the same thing. And, you will notice this if you practice. I know this not only from reading related research studies, but also because I have been a long-term, daily practitioner of mindfulness techniques. I have talked to many others who report the same benefit. Even a few minutes each day will produce a noticeable effect.

*Dealing with General Stress*

Studies which have compared divorce to other life events has shown that people rate it higher, on average, than any other stressor. It is not only a high stressor, but one that does not resolve quickly. Separation stress begins long before your actual separation and continues for years into the future. The most intensely stressful period may be months long.

Chronic stress is bad for your health. The stress hormones in your body which function to make you strong and give you endurance for physical stressors do not help you with emotional or psychological stressors. And, they put you at higher risk of high blood pressure, cardiovascular disease, and immune dysfunction. High-level, chronic stress can exacerbate other diseases. Even if you are not currently fully in control of all the stressful aspects of your life, it is wise to do something to address your overall stress level.

If you are already doing things which help buffer your stress, keep doing them. Many things buffer stress: hobbies, engaging in social activities, volunteering, exercise, yoga, meditation, worship (if you are religious), or playing on a sports team. You may already know of activities which help you release stress. Some may not seem currently ideal due to time or logistical constraints. But, it is important to tailor your lifestyle to include stress-relieving activities.

Some people choose activities which are distracting such as watching television in order to get relief from stress. While I support some activities for that purpose, I encourage you to explore additional activities. Distraction has value, but activities which are merely distracting don't tend to offer the same stress-buffering benefits. Think about the difference between watching a documentary on television about yoga verses attending a twice-weekly yoga class for five weeks. It's fine to use distraction, but do something proactive, too.

Another common strategy for people experiencing chronic stress is to increase tobacco, drug, or alcohol use. I strongly advise against this. No drugs, even legitimate ones prescribed by your doctor, cure the underlying stress. To some extent (perhaps satisfying in some moments), drug use will offer short-term relief from your subjective stress. But, again, doing drugs will function more like a distraction than a proactive stress-relieving activity. And, all drug use comes with risks and costs. If you use drugs as a method for dealing with chronic divorce stress, you will be putting yourself at risk for significant health, monetary, legal, and social issues. Drugs generally interfere with, rather than support, good quality interactions between separated parents. And, drug use can get in the way of safe and effective parenting. You are not likely to ever hear this from an adult whose parents divorced, *You know, my parents handled their divorce OK. But, I really wish they would have been drunk more of the time!*

*Dealing with Short-Term Spikes of Stress*

There will be moments when you are aware that your stress level is spiking. You could think about your stress level on a scale of zero to ten. Perhaps you would report that, over that last few weeks, you are maintaining an average score of around six. You might also report that the lowest your ever feel is about a four and sometimes it spikes up to near ten. Practicing general stress-relieving techniques as discussed in the first section of this chapter will help you lower your average baseline and will also help you achieve a lower bottom score. If you engage in ongoing stress management, you might report in a few weeks that your average is now around five and sometimes as low as two. You will have to actually practice something in order to get that result. And, you will have to practice with dedication since that type of change doesn't tend to happen from one day to the next. But, it is an essential goal, so I strongly encourage it.

In addition to engaging in general stress management, you need to regularly employ short-term strategies to deal with the spikes in your stress level. These short-term techniques will produce that general benefit over time. But, they are very important for their short-term effect. If you have understood my prior explanations about the complicating effects stress has on perception and behavior, then you see the value of being able to reduce stress. This is true even if you are unable to totally remove the stressor. In a co-parenting situation when you are triggered and spiking up to a nine, it will be beneficial for you to be able to come back down, even if only as low as a seven. You would prefer to get lower, but any lowering is going to worth the effort. The good news is that there are many, many such brief techniques and they come with no costs or side effects! I will offer six here. You can find many more online, and I recommend reading *Buddha's Brain* and *Just One Thing* by Rick Hanson or *It's All Well and Good* by Beth Moses for additional strategies.

### Strategy One: Counting

I'm sure you've heard of, or practiced, the technique of counting to ten in a stressful situation. One reason counting works is that, even though it is a very simple cognitive activity, is occupies attention sufficiently to provide short-term distraction from other thoughts. You can only think of one thing at a time. The simple act of counting will prevent you, temporarily, from attending to your stressful thoughts. During the time you are counting, you may come back down a notch or two. The span of time for counting depends on how quickly you are able to come back down. I recommend experimenting with counting to ten, twenty, thirty, or even, forty.

### Strategy Two: Take a Deep Breath

When stress goes up, our breathing often moves up into our chests. Some people even seem to be holding their breath when very stressed. Of course, you need to keep breathing. And, you may benefit from taking a few deep breaths. Try it right now. You already know how to sigh, right? I want you to sigh and then breath in a relaxed manner for a few breaths. Then sigh and relax, again. Do this three times in a row. Three sighs with a few breaths between them. Don't just think about whether this sounds like good advice, actually do it! Do you notice the instant reduction in stress? Most people notice some.

## Strategy Three: Calming Words

This strategy is a modification of a brief meditation technique taught by the Buddhist monk, Thick Nhat Hanh. To perform this meditation, you continue to breathe at your normal rate. Don't try to make your breath any different than it is naturally happening. The goal is not to have any particular type or length of breath. If it becomes more slow and deep, and that feels good, then fine. But, don't struggle with trying to make your breath change. While breathing, you say (quietly, in your head) the following word pairs. Say the first word while breathing in and the second while breathing out.

*In/Out*
*Deep/Slow*
*Calm/Relax*

This technique, like counting, places something in your mind which replaces negative thinking. It also employs words whose meanings point you toward a lower stress level. To get more effect, repeat it three to ten times. Try it right now. Say these words to yourself three times while breathing normally. Notice the relaxation? If not, do it more times through the sequence. This technique can be practiced anywhere but, if possible, you might want to try it while either sitting upright in a chair with your spine straight (not slouching which constrains your abdomen) or while lying down in a relaxed position facing up.

## Strategy Four: Walking Meditation

Walking meditation can be practiced any time you are able to walk without having to be too involved attending to something or someone else. It can be done when you aren't on the phone or having to keep your dog from jumping on strangers. And, it doesn't have to be practiced at a very slow speed. You can walk along at your normal pace (or just slightly slower) and be mindful of your body and breath. There are many methods and you can easily find more online. One method is practiced like this: Merely walk and breathe. When you begin your in-breath, say silently to yourself: In. When you begin to exhale, say: Out. If you take additional steps after saying In or Out, just count up until your breath phase changes to Out or In. It might sound like this in your head: *In, two, three, four, Out, two, three, four, five, In, two, three, four, Out, two, three, four, five...*

Don't worry about counting up to any particular number. Don't try to breath in any unusual way. Just allow your breath to happen normally and try to take a step whenever you begin the in or out phase, then count up. It's that easy. Like the other exercises, the counting gives your brain something to do other than focus on negative thoughts. Being mindful of your breath can be relaxing as well. Many people like this activity because it involves movement, rather than being still.

## Strategy Five: Sitting Meditation

This one involves sitting up straight in a chair in a relaxed position. It is better to sit upright, away from the back of the chair so you are not in a slouching position. Either use a clock or timer, or play one or two songs on your headphones to let you know when the time is finished. If you use songs, choose relaxing songs, preferably with no vocals. Sit for three to ten minutes.

During your sitting period, do two things. First, keep your attention on your breath. Either focus on the movement of your abdomen or on the sensation of air coming in and out of your nose. If your attention wanders (and it likely will), just gently bring it back to your breath. The other thing you can do is say, silently, to yourself, In, with the in-breath, and, Out, with the out-breath.

Breathe naturally. Don't try to change the quality of your breath. If it becomes more relaxed and slow, that's fine. But, just let your breath happen however it feels natural. Practice this method two to four times each day.

Be aware that the goal is not to stop thinking. It is not possible to do so. If you see breath meditation as shutting off your thoughts, you will feel like a failure. You are awake, so your brain will be active. Saying *in* and *out* to yourself gives your brain something to do. But, your brain is designed to seek stimulation, so random thoughts will pop into your head. However, unless the thought is, *I smell smoke and see fire so I should jump out the window*, then allow those thoughts to happen, but don't stick with them. A friend of mine uses the metaphor of waiting for a bus. Watching thoughts appear during meditation is like sitting at a bus stop, but choosing to allow each bus to pass you by. But, if you find yourself somehow on a bus, just get back off at the next stop, sit down, and watch busses passing by, again.

## Strategy Six: Gratitude

Recent research has shown that focusing consciously on things about which we are grateful causes us to unhook from stress and have more positive emotion. Part of the explanation may be that you engage the frontal lobe when you think about positive things. And, engaging the frontal lobe with positive thinking counteracts the stress response. However, it works, you can benefit from this practice. Like the others, it takes little time and has no negative side effects. Do know that this is not a moral or religious practice. If you think that it helps you be a good citizen or religious person, that is fine. But, the technique is offered here because of its emotional and psychological benefits.

Gratitude can be practiced as such. Set a short amount of time to do the exercise. Either set a timer, watch a clock, or listen to a (relaxing) song or two so you when you are finished. Write in a notebook a list of things about which you are grateful. I suggest that rather than thinking hard about the big things in your life and writing a lengthy explanation of your thoughts about them, that you use this more as a brain-storming activity. Just let your mind randomly come up with things. List each one, then open to noticing another. Allow yourself to write things that may seem relatively trivial. If you do this, you relax the editing function of your brain so that you can think of a wider set of things. And, it's OK if you list an item multiple times. Just list each thing as it pops into your head. Do this two to three times each day.

# 10 TYING IT ALL TOGETHER

Co-parenting is complicated, even in the best of situations. Parenting a child together is one of life's most complex set of tasks when parents *aren't* separated. Many post-separation issues make this job even more challenging. This is not news to you. If you are motivated enough to read a book about co-parenting, then you have thought carefully about those challenges and how it ought to be better. I wrote this book because even reasonably functional parents, pointed in the right direction, and taking the right steps, get easily mired in lasting and unsatisfying conflict. This often leads to frustration and a lack of hopefulness. It thwarts, or delays, progress toward crafting a functional co-parenting relationship.

You may be disappointed that this book didn't offer more ways to get your other parent to behave the way you think she or he should. That wasn't the point. **The Co-parenting Manifesto** is a toolbox of strategies to help *you* be the kind of parent you need to be on *your* end of the relationship. You simply aren't in control of your ex. You can run interference for him or her. But, you don't have much leverage to control his or her behaviors.

## Pay Attention to the Brain Effects

This book is about what *you* perceive and how *you* act. As physical beings, you are wired to have predictably skewed perceptions when under stress. And, these shifts in perception have consequential implications for you as a separated parent. The good news is that knowing about the predictable shifts allows you to be more in control. You may not like that the car pulls to the left. But, knowing about it lets you steer safely down the middle of the road. Ignore it (while only wishing it were different) and you'll drive in a big curve off the left side of the road and into the ditch!

Know that even if your brain tells you it is, the building usually *isn't* on fire. Practice sorting issues in terms of importance and urgency and address them, or not, accordingly. Failing to do this will rely on your stress response to guide you. And, we know where that leads. If you are having trouble calming down, at least you can know that you aren't calm. You can see how stress is activating you. You can learn to not deal with things in your worst moments. This is my hope for you.

## Focus on the Process

Certainly, you must deal with substantive issues in your current situation. The focus here on *process* is not to trivialize those issues. However, having talked with thousands of separated parents, I know that process matters. It matters a lot! I trust that parents generally have the capacity to focus competently on issues well if they handle stress and communicate and cooperate more effectively. I believe that you will do that better if you actually focus on how you do it, rather than keeping your attention on the issues, or staying in a reactive, hostile mode.

Have the process conversation. Put the process out on the table so that you and your other parent can work with it, directly. Define it as a shared project, even if your other parent doesn't seem on board the same way you are in this moment.

Know that becoming functional co-parents will be the result of more than good intentions. It will occur only if you and your other parent take many steps to create it. If it has yet to develop in the way that you see as best, don't indict yourself, or your other parent, too quickly. Be aware of your individual, and combined, conflict styles. Explore strategies that help you deal with those style preferences.

## Practice Stress Management Daily

Focusing on and handling stress is essential. Otherwise functional people get into unending conflicts often because they are not able to keep the helpful parts of their brains online during co-parenting interactions. Sure, your ex could change his or her behaviors in ways that lower your stress. But, until he or she does, you must take charge of how stress works in your brain. Understand how it shifts your perceptions and shapes your reactions. Know enough about your own stress response so that you can use that knowledge to steer out of negative, damaging reactions. Get good sleep. Reduce your caffeine intake.

The advice you've found here in *The Co-Parenting Manifesto* is built around putting your in control by reducing the negative effects of stress. Hundreds of studies in the fields of neurology and cognitive science show the many and dramatic ways that stress, and poor sleep, influence your brain state. Many of these effects are very, very unhelpful for a separated parent. And, perhaps one of the worst parts, our brains are wired to view these skewed perceptions as reality. You can counteract these negative effects by lowering your stress.

Many parents ignore my advice to practice stress management

techniques. I understand that people often think they are too busy to take a few minutes per day to devote to something with which they have no experience. They may not be hopeful that such a simple activity can result in such a positive result. And, it's true, some of the results don't seem to emerge until you've practiced the techniques for some time. But, please do experiment with stress management— either the techniques I've described in the book, or others that you find in other books or site. If you don't, you're throwing away the most powerful part of this book. If you choose to not practice a few minutes of stress management daily for a few weeks and decide that this program doesn't work for you then you are making that choice without sufficient information. Try it for a few weeks, then stop if it isn't working.

Try it right now, once again. Take a deep breath and let it out in a long, slow, sigh. How did that feel? That probably took you under thirty seconds. And, it provided immediate, noticeable stress relief. Explore some techniques that you can do for just a few minutes a few times each day. Do these in moments when you need to calm down or prepare for a stressful interaction. But, also do them in order to progressively rewire your brain toward a more calm, centered state.

### Don't Give Up Too Soon!

It will take some time to realize a more ideal co-parenting relationship. Remember that I have explained multiple brain effects that result in your having an overly negative set of perceptions. And, there are artifacts of your past stress that will come along with you, even if you are behaving perfectly. Also, your ex will seem to you to not be behaving better for some time, even if she or he actually is. You will be perceived by your ex as behaving more badly than you actually are. This means that you must both behave better *and* persevere! Stick with it!

## Cut Yourselves Some Slack

You and your ex are involved in the most complicated and stressful set of tasks of your entire lives. Cut yourselves some slack. Chill out! If it seems wildly challenging and stressful, that's because *it is*! You are having accurate perceptions, there. Should you work to make it better? Yes. But, the most functional parents on the planet, pointed in the right direction, and taking the right steps don't instantly solve all their co-parenting complications in one day. The fact that you haven't gotten there, yet, doesn't mean you won't make progress.

## My Ex is Evil, Stupid, & Crazy!

Give it up. You can think this. It's completely normal. You can express this to your therapist, or best friend (only when your children are not present). But, stop expressing this set of thoughts to your children or your other parent. It is unhelpful and damaging. I don't care if it's true. Stop it. Stop expressing this with your words and behaviors.

This way of thinking perpetuates attachment, judging, and complaining. None of that is helpful. It makes you less responsible. It promotes hostility. It makes you more likely to dump more stress on your child rather than nurture them and help them cope with their own stress.

The antidote to this is to use *clean language*. Not everything has to do with your separation, even if your brain tells you that it does. Learn to catch this negative thinking and express something more neutral. Your children will thank you for this a couple of decades from now. But, even if they never get around to it, do it, anyway.

## Bless You for Your Courage & Strength

I have had the wonderful opportunity over the last fifteen years to work with hundreds, and speak to thousands, of separated parents. This is wonderful because of the courage and strength I have seen expressed in so many ways by so many parents. I am blessed to have had the chance to connect with parents and go to their particular hells with them. It is my sincere hope that, at least some of the time, I have helped them with those hells. If some of this book resonates with you, may it help you transform some of your separation and parenting hell into something that works for you and your child. I have faith that it can. But, it will be as a result of your courage and strength. Bless you for that. Parenting is hard, no matter what your circumstances. Right now, yours are challenging. Good luck!

# ABOUT THE AUTHOR

Jon Peters, MSW is a clinical social worker and has worked with separated parents for over fifteen years. He is the author of *The Quick Guide to Divorce Mediation*. He has worked as a therapist, mediator, coach, custody evaluator, parenting coordinator, and expert witness in hundreds of cases. As a divorce educator, he has delivered more than two hundred divorce classes to over five thousand parents. He has delivered more than fifty-five undergraduate and graduate university courses concerning mental health, addiction, research theory and methodology, and stress management.

To contact Jon: www.coparentingbetter.com

Printed in Great Britain
by Amazon